D0059865

DR. FEELGOOD

Copyright © 2013 by Richard A. Lertzman and William J. Birnes

All Rights Reserved. No part of this book may be reproduced in any manner without the express written consent of the publisher, except in the case of brief excerpts in critical reviews or articles. All inquiries should be addressed to Skyhorse Publishing, 307 West 36th Street, 11th Floor, New York, NY 10018.

Skyhorse Publishing books may be purchased in bulk at special discounts for sales promotion, corporate gifts, fund-raising, or educational purposes. Special editions can also be created to specifications. For details, contact the Special Sales Department, Skyhorse Publishing, 307 West 36th Street, 11th Floor, New York, NY 10018 or info@skyhorsepublishing.com.

Skyhorse® and Skyhorse Publishing® are registered trademarks of Skyhorse Publishing, Inc.®, a Delaware corporation.

Visit our website at www.skyhorsepublishing.com.

10 9 8 7 6 5 4 3

Library of Congress Cataloging-in-Publication Data is available on file.
ISBN: 978-1-62087-589-6

Printed in the United States of America

DR. FEELGOOD

The Shocking Story
of the Doctor
Who May Have
Changed History
by Treating
and Drugging
JFK, Marilyn,
Elvis, and Other
Prominent Figures

Richard A. Lertzman and William
J. Birnes

Skyhorse Publishing

Contents

Acknowledgments

The journey to write this book took us throughout the United States and allowed us to talk to many individuals who were cogent of Dr. Max Jacobson. The authors lived peripatetic lives in our explorations for the truth. The kind generosity of these contributors allowed us to paint a picture of this mysterious physician who had purposely shrouded his life even as he wound a web of addiction from New York, through Washington, to Los Angeles, entrapping his patients in a downward spiral of self-destructive behaviors.

The story began with the intent to document the life of actor Robert Cummings, one of the most important A-list screen and television celebrities of the 1940s and '50s, who wound up desperately broke and alone in an old age home in the San Fernando Valley as a result of his addiction to Dr. Feelgood's methamphetamine injections. But as we began to understand the reach of Dr. Feelgood, his relationship with the Kennedys, the Sam Giancana's organized crime family, and with Frank Sinatra's Rat Pack, we knew that this was a far bigger story than we had originally planned to write. We realized that Dr. Feelgood was a part of twentieth-century American political history and his story needed to be documented.

Our research was benefited by many people. We offer plaudits and thanks to those who have helped make this book a reality, especially, first and foremost, the late author C. David Heymann and his wife Bea Schwartz, who helped us with important facts and set us on our course in the right direction. Our other inspiration was actor and director Dwayne Hickman, who, though best known for portraying "Dobie Gillis" on television, was also a friend of Bob Cummings, who told us the first stories about Max Jacobson. We thank Joan Roberts for her support, as well.

Further acknowledgments go to to Melinda Cummings Cameron and her husband Professor Kim Cameron; television icon Art Linkletter and his wife Lois; Pamela Shoop; actress Julie Newmar; the late singer Andy Williams and press agent Paul Shefrin; journalist Seymour Hersh; socialite Tony Bradlee; Jill Jacobson and her youngest son, Matthew; the late psychiatrist Dr. Lawrence Hatterer; the late Michael Samek; actor Roscoe Lee Browne; playwright Alvin Aronson; physician and pioneering astronaut Dr. David Simons; JFK Secret Service agent Paul Landis; the late Tony Curtis; legendary television and motion picture star Jerry Lewis; singer Phyllis McGuire; the late actress Alice Ghostley; television writers and producers Rocky and Irma Kalish; late television producer Bob Finkel; *Hustler* magazine owner and publisher Larry Flynt; writer and producer of *The Twilight Zone* Del Reisman; film editor Stanley Frazen; actress Eileen Wesson; actress Linda Henning; film director Sam Irvin; the late astrologer Sidney Omar; the late Hollywood photographer Wallace Seawell; Patricia Cummings; talk show host and comedian Joey Bishop; actor Jamie Farr; comedy writer Larry Gelbart (*Oh, God, Tootsie,* and *M*A*S*H*); Gary Owens; actor William Schallert; actor Ed Asner; the late film and television director/writer Hal Kanter; the late writer Irving Brecher; the late TV legend Milton Berle and his son Bill Berle; the late producer and writer Leonard Stern; legendary head of the William Morris Agency-Norm Brokaw; super agent Jay Kanter; the late actor Bob Easton; critic writer Shawn Levy; Valentina Quinn, daughter of actor Anthony Quinn; the late singer Eddie Fisher; film director Robert Child (*Silent Wings*); and actress Ann B. Davis.

We offer a debt of gratitude to pharmacology expert, writer, and Oxford Professor Leslie Iverson; writer Roger Rappoport (*The Super Doctors*); author Nina Burleigh (*A Very Private Woman*); author and Professor Robert Dallek; writer Tania Grossinger (*Growing up at Grossingers*); David and Juliet Shaw (son of Mark Shaw); writer and journalist Jane Leavy (*The Last Boy: Mickey Mantle*); writer Curt Smith (*The Voice: Mel Allen*); writer A.E. Hotchner (and co-founder with Paul Newman of "Newman's Own" brands); animal activist and national television and radio pet expert Tracy Hotchner; Laurel Cummings Jones; writer Linda Jay Geldens (*Rod Serling*); Washington Internist and author Dr. Jeffrey Kelman; *New York Times* journalists Jane Brody; Lawrence Altman, and Boyce Rensberger; writer Frederick Kempe (*Berlin 1961*); writer Gore Vidal; writers and historians Lawrence Leamer and Nigel Hamilton; Broadway producer (with Alan Jay Lerner) Bud Widney; actor Jason Wingreen; Robert Cummings, Jr.; actress Pat Suzuki (*Flower Drum Song*, the former wife of Mark Shaw); actress Rose Marie; former First Lady Nancy Reagan; film and television director William Asher; Tom Putnam (director of the John F. Kennedy Presidential Library and Museum); and countless others who were of great assistance in the creation of this book.

For Richard Lertzman, I'd like to thank my son Matthew David Lertzman for his great assistance and being a loyal travel companion on this adventure.

For Bill Birnes, I want to dedicate this work to my godfathers, Nathan Birnbaum (who once told me to forget everything I was doing and make a movie), and Benjamin Kubelsky, who, ironically, after a century, were both responsible for much of the show business history we describe in this book. And to the Gruskin/Birnes Agency, the inventors of show business merchandise licensing. And finally to "The Burns Brothers," an early vaudeville song-and-dance team, and to "The Chicken Sisters," who performed on the *Jack Benny Program* on radio.

Preface

When you approach a story, no matter how sensational it seems on the surface, the more you explore its ramifications, the twists it takes, and the bends it makes, the more you come to appreciate and understand the larger picture. This is exactly what we discovered as we uncovered the story of Dr. Max Jacobson, an individual who, in some fundamental ways, influenced American history, even if his influence was tangential rather than immediately intentional. What we discovered and what we want to establish beyond the sensationalism of this story is how a single individual, Max Jacobson, became a lightning rod for any entity—public, political, or commercial—that wanted to use him because of a synthesized drug he developed that behaves like a fast-spreading virus. He became a drug addict after he injected himself with his own methamphetamine-laced concoctions, and he addicted others, propelled by a psychosis that came from the methamphetamine itself. Even more than a sensational story, this is a fascinating case study of how human connections form, spread, and deteriorate so as to change the course of history. What Max Jacobson did still affects us today in how the press operates and in our war on drugs.

When we looked at the totality of Max Jacobson's effect on American culture—albeit having started inside a niche segment of that culture—the lives that were destroyed or otherwise influenced, and the spread of Max Jacobson's influence across cultural lines, we realized we were looking at more than a story about a drug; we were looking at a type of social phenomenon, something that British scientist and author Richard Dawkins[1] might call a "meme," which was working its way through a social network that Max Jacobson helped create. But we soon found that this was more than something Max Jacobson created. Because Jacobson himself was an addict controlled by methamphetamine, it was the drug that had become the meme. It remains today as a party drug of choice, though it's ingested in a different form. We found that all the way from a popular Aretha Franklin song about Dr. Feelgood, to a Blake Edwards motion picture that featured a meth-injecting doctor at Hollywood parties, to serious political histories by Seymour Hersh and Robert Dallek, Max Jacobson had merely been portrayed as an anecdotal cultural footnote when, in fact, he was the spear point of a cultural change in America. And that is what this book documents.

Our study of the infamous Dr. Feelgood, Dr. Max Jacobson, had a narrow beginning as a show-business biography of motion picture and television star Robert Cummings, who was widely known as one of the first health food advocates in Hollywood and who had written a hugely successful book, *How to Stay Young and Vital*, in 1960 that sold millions of copies. We started out to write the story of how this self-described "clean living" popular figure, who had starred in Alfred Hitchcock's *Dial M for Murder* and *Saboteur* and costarred with Ronald Reagan, fell into a precipitous decline because of his addiction to Max Jacobson's drug cocktail. As our interviews circled out from actor Dwayne

Hickman, of *The Many Loves of Dobie Gillis* fame and Cummings's co-star in *Love That Bob,* we realized that Cummings's relationship with Jacobson mirrored Jacobson's relationships with many show-business figures, artists, and even key political figures such as President Kennedy. We realized we were on the trail of a larger story about how some of America's most influential personalities from the 1940s to the 1970s were influenced by a drug and the provider of that drug.

As we talked to other celebrities of that period, former Jacobson patients, and historians who shared their own records with us, we realized our story about Bob Cummings may become the story of Jack and Jackie Kennedy. Soon, such figures as J. Edgar Hoover, Senator Claude Pepper, vice president Spiro Agnew, and even presidents Richard Nixon and Harry Truman became involved. Who was Max Jacobson? And how did the drug he synthesized exert so much influence? What was really at work as the drug spread, and how had it remained under the radar for more than thirty years, only to emerge in a headline-making story on the pages of the *New York Times* and in the news broadcasts of a crusading young Geraldo Rivera?

To find the truths behind the Max Jacobson story, we have traveled throughout the United States to interview American legends from all walks of life, Max Jacobson's patients, and family members and friends of patients. We learned that Jacobson's influence extended worldwide and that his drug cocktail affected the lives of some of the most influential leaders of the twentieth century.

Our pursuit to research the life and denouement of Max Jacobson began in Branson, Missouri, with an interview with singer Andy Williams, then to Washington, D.C., for conversations with journalist Sy Hersh and socialite Tony Bradlee, the sister of ex-JFK mistress Mary Pinchot Meyer. Then, after researching FBI and CIA public documents, we met with C. David Heymann in Manhattan. In New York, we also spoke to noted psychiatrist Dr. Lawrence Hatterer, who treated President Kennedy at New York's Carlyle Hotel after an injection from Max Jacobson that so overdosed the president he began running naked through the halls of the hotel. We also spoke to Max Jacobson's best friend, World War II hero and Medal of Honor recipient Michael Samek, a chemical engineer who understood what Max was mixing up in his lab and tried to help him organize his business, even as New York state authorities were closing in.

The list of former patients and celebrities who were friends of patients was extensive and included show business icons Jerry Lewis, Tony Curtis, George Clooney, Roscoe Lee Browne singer Phyllis McGuire, actresses Alice Ghostley and Julie Newmar, Ed Asner, William Schallert of *The Patty Duke Show,* the late Art Linkletter, our friend Dwayne Hickman, comedian Joey Bishop, actor Jamie Farr from *M*A*S*H*, comedy writer Larry Gelbart, television legend Milton Berle, and many others—more than we can mention here.

Our research also included medical doctors, pharmacology experts, and Max Jacobson's son, Dr. Thomas Jacobson. Interviews also included writers Roger Rapoport (*The Super-Doctors*), Nina Burleigh (*A Very Private Woman,* about the death of Mary Pinchot Meyer), professor and Kennedy scholar Robert Dallek, writer and journalist Jane Leavy (*The Last Boy: Mickey Mantle*), writer Curt Smith (*The Voice: Mel Allen*), and famed writer A. E. Hotchner, who cofounded the Newman's Own food brand with Paul Newman.

Just reviewing the list of Max Jacobson's patients in the appendix will give you an understanding of the breadth of Jacobson's reach and the level of research into medical files and the depth of the interviews. Information from the *New York Times's* Jane Brody, Lawrence Altman, Boyce Rensberger, writer Frederick Kempe (Berlin 1961), historian Lawrence Leamer, and writer Gore Vidal provided much-needed background about Jacobson and his patients within the context of American cultural history from 1940 through the early 1970s.

We wondered how many other lives were destroyed by this supposed vitamin cocktail that was supplied by the person the Secret Service code-named "Dr. Feelgood." How had this German immigrant impacted American history? We relied on information provided by the late C. David Heymann, who had extensively interviewed John F. Kennedy, Jr., and whose research into the influence of Max Jacobson on both President Kennedy and Jackie Kennedy made him aware of the dark secret that ran like an underground stream through Camelot.

We learned far more than we bargained for, particularly discovering that heroes of our generation, cultural icons, and the screen and television actors who influenced our outlook on life were, after all, still human beings plagued with many of the shortcomings that plague the rest of us. We learned the dark truths about the final weeks of Marilyn Monroe, J. Edgar Hoover's secret addiction to methamphetamines, Mickey Mantle's use of performance-enhancing drugs as well as his reliance on Max Jacobson during the Mick's homerun derby with Yankee teammate Roger Maris, and the solution to the Mary Meyer murder in Georgetown and her shared drug addiction with the president, to whom she brought LSD tabs from her friend Dr. Timothy Leary, all under the watchful eyes of James Jesus Angelton of the CIA.

The full story of Dr. Max Jacobson, his influence, his medicines, his rise and fall, and how he became a useful tool for the KGB, the CIA, the New York State Board of Regents, and the American national media has never been told until now. As jaded as we are, we admit to having been completely astonished.

DR. FEELGOOD

Introduction

On December 3, 1979, funeral services were held for Dr. Max Jacobson at the Frank E. Campbell Funeral Chapel at Madison Avenue at 81st Street in his adopted hometown of New York City. The Campbell Chapel has been the home of countless notable funerals, including those held for Irving Berlin, Joan Crawford, Bat Masterson, Judy Garland, Walter Cronkite, Rudolph Valentino, Tennessee Williams, mob boss Frank Costello, and many others. Jacobson's was a traditional Jewish memorial followed by a shiva, a Jewish mourning period in which the deceased's family receives condolences at home. Jacobson's friend Michael Samek remembered that the funeral was well attended and that Jacobson was buried at Mt. Hebron Cemetery, which is in Queens, New York, next to his wife Nina and his parents, Louis and Ernestine. The celebrities in attendance at Dr. Jacobson's funeral attested to the doctor's extensive influence in the entertainment industry, among artists and writers, and in the world of politics and government.

The impact of the life and practices of Dr. Max Jacobson has reverberated for decades. There have been more than two hundred books touching on Jacobson, his drugs, and the lives he destroyed.

Some of these books were written by patients who knew him intimately (such as Doris Shapiro's *We Danced All Night* and Eddie Fisher's *Been There, Done That*), while others were written by historians and popular writers (such as Roger Rapoport's *The Super-Doctors*, which takes a deeper look at Jacobson within a medical and historical context). Movies such as Blake Edwards's *S.O.B.* have parodied him, and songs such as Aretha Franklin's "Dr. Feelgood" have immortalized him. The deaths of former patients have been blamed on him, such as Jackie Kennedy's fatal lymphoma, and actor Bob Cummings's decline and his death from Parkinson's disease. There were many other deaths including Kennedy family photographer and Jacobson's friend Mark Shaw, Alan J. Lerner, and Max's own wife, Nina.

Whether lionized or vilified by his patients, Dr. Max Jacobson has become a part of the fabric of the twentieth century. There have been credible studies of his impact on John F. Kennedy, Jr. by popular historians such as Robert Dallek, Seymour Hersh, Richard Reeves, Frederick Kempe, C. David Heymann, Barbara Leaming, and Lawrence Leamer, all of whom reported that JFK's life was deeply influenced by his relationship with Jacobson. The internet is replete with conspiracy theories surrounding Jacobson. Radio talk show hosts have held discussions on the "Jacobson Effect." His nickname, Dr. Feelgood, is now commonly used to refer to numerous modern doctors whose misuse of drugs caused their patients harm or death, such as the late Michael Jackson's physician Dr. Conrad Murray. Even the widespread use of methamphetamines in the United States has been blamed on Jacobson. Dr. Leslie Iversen, one of the leading experts on amphetamine use and a professor of pharmacology at Oxford University, directly links Jacobson's drug practices to the current spread of methamphetamines.

Ironically, despite all his influence and notoriety, Max Jacobson did not become a rich man by any account. Claims, such as the one made by actor Felice Orlandi, that Jacobson ran a global amphetamine syndicate that made millions of dollars were not borne out by reality. Jacobson himself complained that the legal defense he raised before the state of New York was so expensive, he was afraid it might wipe him out. In their exposé of Jacobson published on December 4, 1972, Rensenberger, Brody, and Altman of the *New York Times* wrote that despite Max Jacobson's rich clientele of patients, he lived very modestly in what could be called a middle-class apartment.

His best friend, Michael Samek, noted that "Max never got rich. He never set up a proper billing system. He was never paid by many patients and that includes President Kennedy. . . . Max was a very compassionate person. He wanted to help his patients. Max always said, 'It's better to feel good than to feel sick.' Treating patients was his life—not money. He saw his practice as a sort of mission."[2] The debate continues as to whether Jacobson was a fraud and a charlatan or a cutting-edge and compassionate physician. As fascinating as Jacobson's story is in and of itself, it is also the story of methamphetamine, a drug that deludes those who use it into thinking they are larger than life. The drug is a Venus flytrap that lures, entraps, and then finally kills its victims.

On a positive note, medical licensing laws changed because of Jacobson. The War on Drugs emerged, in a small measure, out of the scandal surrounding Jacobson. Because of the influence he wielded with a drug that frightened federal secret intelligence agencies, conspirators within those agencies took extreme measures to protect power they felt belonged to them.

Jacobson was not only an instrument of destruction—inadvertently as well as deliberately as he sought to exert his control over those around him—but he also was a tool used by the media to sell newspapers as the Nixon administration crumbled from within. He was vilified not just in the print and broadcast media, but by New York State regulators, who revoked his license to practice medicine as they made an example of a person they believed had abused every aspect of medical procedure when it came to preparing and dispensing medication. In a larger sense, too, Max Jacobson became the poster boy for drug abuse, and in the wake of his exposure, the federal government created and then prosecuted its War on Drugs.

Perhaps the most ironic aspect of the Max Jacobson story was the way it demonstrated how human networks formed, how a drug addiction can spread virally among specific groups, and how an individual at the center of that network, just like a spider, can weave and spread his web to ensnare others. Indeed, we can call the Jacobson story a tragedy, but it's an illustrative tragedy showcasing the ways human beings influence others so as to create an entire social movement. As grandiose as this sounds, it's true.

Chapter 1

JFK and Dr. Max Jacobson in Camelot

"If you look backwards, you face the future with your ass."
—Dr. Max Jacobson

"Mrs. Dunn is calling," the office receptionist announced.

A hunched-over, bespectacled man in a dirty, bloodstained lab coat looked up from under a curl of thick black hair, first at the syringe he was holding and then at his receptionist, and nodded. No matter what he was doing, Dr. Max Jacobson would take the call. "Mrs. Dunn" always took precedence.

"Mrs. Dunn" was John Fitzgerald Kennedy, the thirty-fifth president of the United States. "Dunn" was the code name concocted by the president and the mysterious doctor from their earliest encounters. Ever since the first televised debate in the 1960 presidential campaign, Max Jacobson had become JFK's unofficial doctor, keeping him upright, functioning, and invigorated. But it was a tightly kept secret, hidden from the American public and—as much as possible—from the press corps that followed the young president everywhere he went. No American could know that his president was calling on a doctor who had fled the Nazi takeover of Germany and worked out of a small, cluttered Upper East Side Manhattan office to summon him to the White House, where from time to time he received "special" injections. And Dr. Max Jacobson, although proud of what he was doing, dutifully kept the secret.

Jacobson was on the radar of both the CIA and the FBI, not simply because of his proximity to JFK, but because in the eyes of these intelligence and counterespionage services, he had become a person of interest. In addition to his association with known communist agents, Jacobson was also treating CIA officers. Among those officers was former OSS officer and JFK family photographer Mark Shaw. Both FBI and CIA interest only intensified when Jack Kennedy's old college roommate, Chuck Spalding, introduced Jacobson to the then-Democratic candidate for president, whom Max began treating in 1960. As a consequence of Max's associations and his new relationship with JFK, his office was placed under surveillance.

FBI surveillance of Max's office noted, as did a reference in the CIA file, that Dr. Jacobson was treating an affluent, highly circumscribed clientele of patients, most of whom were connected to the arts. Although there was no speculation regarding the nature of Max's treatments, both agencies remarked that Max's high-profile clientele were devoted followers of the doctor. However, in at least one note in Max's FBI file, the agency said that although Max described himself as a researcher for treating multiple sclerosis, the FBI noted that the multiple sclerosis society referred to Jacobson as a "quack" and a "charlatan," a complaint that would later be lodged against him by Mark Shaw's ex-wife Gerrit Trotta.[3]

On a Sunday in February 1963, Jacobson's office was nearly destroyed by a "break-in." Papers were removed, medical vials were missing, and the office was completely trashed. It had been assumed that the "raid" came from the FBI. When we acquired the FBI files through FOIA, there was much that was redacted and missing. JFK's orthopedic specialist, Dr. Han Kraus, suffered a similar break-in. His Manhattan office was ransacked once, which President Kennedy and others blamed on J. Edgar Hoover, who was compiling a file on the Kennedys for his own purposes of self-protection. Robert Kennedy had made no bones about wanting to replace Hoover at the FBI, even talking to police chief William H. Parker in Los Angeles about taking over the Bureau. Dr. Kraus wisecracked, "Even if Hoover had gotten his hands on Kennedy's files [which he didn't], all that would have happened is that he would have discovered that Kennedy did exercises."

Ken McKnight recalled, "The Food and Drug Administration was on Max's back the whole time I knew him. After he began treating JFK and he became president, the FBI also began snooping around."

Code-named "Dr. Feelgood" by the Secret Service detail guarding the president, Max Jacobson was an omnipresent figure among those surrounding President Kennedy and First Lady Jacqueline during the two-and-a-half years they occupied the White House. Jacobson and his wife had accompanied the president to meet Charles de Gaulle in Paris and would also be present at the Vienna summit with Soviet premier Nikita Khrushchev in June 1961. The Jacobsons attended the president's birthday party at Madison Square Garden and were frequent visitors at the Kennedy compound at Hyannis Port, at the West Palm Beach winter White House, and at other celebrations. But only a select few, including the president's brother, Attorney General Robert F. Kennedy, actually knew what was at the core of the president's relationship with Dr. Jacobson.

It was the medicine, and the president was addicted to it.

As would be revealed decades later in a nasty hearing before the New York state medical licensing board and an exposé in the *New York Times*, Max Jacobson's magic elixir was a concoction of different types of blood serum mixed with a powerful methamphetamine stimulant. This mixture of liquid methamphetamines injected directly into the president's bloodstream gave the president, who suffered constant pain from back injuries, a reliable source of energy and a mental high. But, as JFK, Jackie, Marilyn Monroe, and scores of Dr. Jacobson's other patients would ultimately discover, what "Miracle Max," as he was nicknamed by singer Eddie Fisher, touted as his liquid vitamin cocktail actually came at a huge cost. A regimen of methamphetamine resulted in severe neuropsychological reactions, including manic depression or bipolar disorder, hypersexuality, and paranoid hypergrandiosity. In President Kennedy's case, that reaction caused the almost stupor-like depression that he fell into while coming down from his meth high during the Vienna summit with Khrushchev and set into motion the chain of events that would ultimately cost him his own life.

Max Jacobson's connection to the Kennedys began in 1960, when one of Jacobson's patients, Chuck Spalding, Kennedy's former roommate at Harvard, placed a very confidential phone call to him to request a private consultation on behalf of an unidentified friend. This "friend" was in a tight situation, Spalding said, and needed Jacobson's medical advice. Jacobson had been introduced to Spalding by internationally known fashion photographer Mark Shaw, who was another of his patients. Jacobson had in turn met Shaw through his longtime friend, World War II Army Air Force glider pilot Lt. Col. Mike Samek, whose wife was an editor at New

York's *Mademoiselle* magazine. Shaw, like Samek, had been an officer in the OSS during the war and, like most members of the American clandestine services, never left the profession. From the OSS, Shaw had become a nonofficial cover officer, or NOC, for the CIA, a job that required complete anonymity, a "legend," or a cover profession to mask what he really did, and the ability to insinuate himself into critical relationships to send intelligence information back to the agency.

As an internationally recognized photographer, Shaw had almost unlimited access to the popularly termed jet-set of the 1950s by virtue of his acclaimed magazine spreads featuring Audrey Hepburn, Pablo Picasso, Brigitte Bardot, Elizabeth Taylor, Danny Kaye, Grace Kelly, Cary Grant, Yves St. Laurent, and countless other high-profile notables in art, literature, and show business around the world. But the 1950s was also the decade of the Red Scare and the blacklist. With Senator Joseph McCarthy's hearings stoking the flames of fear, the American public became obsessively paranoid over the threat of Communist infiltration of American institutions, especially in the entertainment industry and halls of government. Mark Shaw, therefore, was the consummate fly on the wall, snapping away his photos and privy to intimate conversations held in unguarded moments, conversations of which he took very careful note.

Shaw also presented an additional opportunity to his handlers at the CIA. Because of his relationship with friends in high places, Shaw had established a relationship with the Kennedys and ultimately became the official Kennedy family photographer after JFK won the 1960 election. But, before that, Mark Shaw introduced his old friend Chuck Spalding to Dr. Jacobson. Soon Spalding, as well as Shaw, would become addicted to the substance in Max's magic injections. Thus, when Jack Kennedy called and complained of his lack of stamina during the campaign, Spalding placed the confidential phone call asking Max to consult with the then-Massachusetts senator, who was running for president against vice president Richard M. Nixon.

It was in the early fall of 1960, just before the celebrated, first-televised presidential Kennedy-Nixon debate, when Spalding made the call. "Can you handle this consultation with utmost secrecy?" Spalding asked before finally identifying his former roommate by name. It was vital that Jacobson take extreme steps to avoid any public scrutiny. The last thing JFK needed was to be spotted visiting this strange Manhattan doctor. JFK had already been outed in the media over his health issues, and his campaign staff had spent time dispelling those potentially harmful rumors. Kennedy-the-candidate's Addison's disease, constant back pain, high stress, migraines, and gastrointestinal disorders all had to be kept secret from the public.

There was acute vigilance by the Kennedy staff to keep JFK's illnesses under the radar. JFK's father, Joseph Kennedy, had carefully guarded this secret from the moment his son became a congressman and later passed this duty on to son Bobby. However, in May 1962, rumors swirled that JFK was under the care of Dr. Jacobson. *Esquire* magazine's managing editor, Harold Hayes, commissioned writer and Jacobson patient Arthur Steuer to do a story about JFK's employing Dr. Jacobson as his physician. Jacobson, who by 1962 felt secure in his position with JFK and was not shy at boasting about his treatment of the president, told Steuer of his relationship and history with the president. This caused a flap in the media that had to be quieted; the Kennedy advisors strongly believed that any leak of the president's illness would weaken the office of the president and strongly derail his influence, and Jacobson was later scolded for his loose talk.[1]

The task fell to none other than Mrs. Kennedy's chief of staff and social secretary Letitia Baldrige, who responded to Mr. Steuer's inquiry on White House letterhead, saying that her brother, Howard Malcolm Baldrige, Jr., a former secretary of commerce, was going to use Dr. Jacobson for his Marie-Strumpell disease, implying that it was not JFK who would receive treatment from the doctor.[2] But, despite any cover-ups to the press, it was John F. Kennedy who invited Dr. Jacobson to the White House to treat him and Jackie, and it was he who ultimately asked Jacobson to move into the White House so he could be close at hand.

But none of what was in the future was evident in the summer of 1960 when JFK had his first meeting with Jacobson. At that time, Senator Kennedy was perceived by the media to be a youthful and vigorous naval war hero. The cover-up of the senator's poor health was in full steam during the campaign, even though rumors were circulating concerning his wartime injuries and bad back. On July 5, 1960, Kennedy physicians Dr. Janet Travell and Dr. Eugene J. Cohen sent a signed letter to JFK for public dissemination that was created specifically for those they called the "media vultures,"[3] in which they flatly denied that the senator was in ill health. The letter stated, "As your physicians for over five years and [with] knowledge of your medical records for over 15 years, we wish to provide you with a straightforward brief medical statement concerning your health. . . . As stated to you in our recent letter of 6/11/60 we reiterate that you are in superb physical condition . . . you should see your doctors once or twice a year for a routine check-up . . . no limitations are placed on your arduous activities . . ." This letter was distributed to targeted friends in the press. It was an utter fabrication and a complete cover-up of Senator John Kennedy's physical condition.

With the old-line establishment physicians Travell and Cohen protecting the Kennedy mystique from the press, JFK looked below the radar to find relief from the persistent pain that was draining his strength and causing him great fatigue. Not unlike Michael Jackson, who sought out willing physicians to ease his pain, Kennedy reached out to his friends to find his own sub rosa doctor. And he found him on New York's Upper East Side.

Unlike the upscale and fashionable office of Dr. Travell on West 16th Street, just north of New York's Greenwich Village and only a few blocks away from Union Square, Max's East 72nd Street office in Manhattan was not a typical medical practice. It was more like a research lab with a celebrity waiting room. Actress Alice Ghostley's husband Felice Orlandi, who worked as Max's assistant for several years in the 1960s, remembered that Jacobson's "office was often a complete and utter disaster area. Papers were all over the office, waste cans were overfilled, syringes were strewn across the floor, empty vials were everywhere. He was too cheap to hire a cleaning service. His back lab was like a war zone. Max muttered and mumbled quite a bit. He reminded me a bit like Vincent Price in one of his horror films. His fingernails were just absolutely filthy and he reeked of tobacco and formaldehyde."[4] Jacobson's close friend Mike Samek concurred about the office: "I tried to impress upon Max to clean up the office. In fact, I spent a weekend with a neighborhood kid and we built a wall of shelving in his lab to restore order. It even had slots where he could label the ingredients. Max had a perverse sense of humor and enjoyed the clutter.

He claimed that there was an organization to the disorganization. There was very little regulation by the state in that time."[5]

A frequent Jacobson patient, singer Eddie Fisher, later recalled that "the office looked more like a chemist's laboratory than a doctor's office and Max looked like a mad scientist, I guess. I remember noticing at our first meeting that his fingernails were filthy, stained with chemicals. He was nothing like any other doctor I'd ever met. He was a German refugee, with big thick glasses, a big thick accent, and a completely commanding personality."[6]

Jacobson, who was sixty years old when he met Senator Kennedy, was still a robust man. He was a dedicated swimmer who stayed in good physical condition by doing multiple laps every morning. He had been an amateur boxer and studied jujitsu. He was barrel chested and quite muscular but had a prominent pot belly and cut "a hulking, disheveled figure . . . [with] large horn-rimmed glasses with thick lenses [that] magnified roaming, unsettled eyes."[7]

After taking the phone call from Chuck Spalding, Jacobson became anxious. A promised relationship with a politically prominent patient was as mysterious as it was exciting. Late that same afternoon, the senator showed up. The office, which was usually jam-packed with celebrity patients such as Truman Capote, Tennessee Williams, Alan Jay Lerner, and Anthony Quinn, was now deserted. Jacobson had cleared all of them out.

Just as Spalding had promised to his former roommate, the doctor was gracious, but he stared at the young Democratic presidential candidate through the eyes of a physician as well a civilian basking in the glow of the senator's charismatic presence. Jacobson stared long and hard because he believed that by looking directly into someone's eyes, he could learn everything there was to learn about the person. He was impressed by Kennedy's earnestness and what he perceived to be the candidate's clarity. He noted every aspect of Kennedy's physical condition even before they spoke. In his own records, Jacobson remembered JFK as especially thin, with long fatigue lines in his face and sagging cheeks.

The candidate said that he had given the slip to his security personnel because, as he made clear, he wanted complete anonymity. Jacobson reassured him that he would absolutely keep all their conversations confidential.

Although Senator Kennedy tried to be affable as he stood uncomfortably in Jacobson's office, the doctor could tell he was put off by the cramped space and Jacobson's disheveled appearance. To break the tension, Kennedy began by making small talk about Mark Shaw, who had just been put on a special assignment to photograph Kennedy and his family. Kennedy said that both Shaw and Chuck Spalding had spoken very highly of Jacobson's medical procedures, which had helped them overcome the intense strain of their professions. Both of them had recommended that Kennedy pay Jacobson a visit after a brutal primary campaign against senators Hubert Humphrey and Lyndon Johnson that left him in need of a jumpstart now that the general election campaign was in full swing.

What was Kennedy's medical complaint? Jacobson, ever the skilled diagnostician, asked this while peering at his new patient. It was the demands of the campaign, Kennedy explained. It was draining him. He was fatigued. His muscles felt weak. And this weakness was interfering with his concentration and his speech. Worse, he was getting laryngitis. He was looking ahead to a series of televised debates with his opponent, Vice President Nixon—a fierce and seasoned debater, a street fighter who was known to go after his opponents' jugulars. Kennedy was worried, and the strain

was taking its toll. Even though they had been friends and colleagues in the United States Senate, Kennedy had no illusions about
how Nixon would go after him in the debates.

Jacobson was not at all surprised by Kennedy's description of
his physical problems. The senator's complaints, however, consti-
tuted the most common symptoms of stress, which, in Jacobson's
opinion, if not addressed, would only become more severe. He
took a short case history, asking the presidential candidate about
any previous diseases he had contracted, accidents or injuries from
the war, and treatments he had been given. JFK started by describing his Addison's disease, and how it resulted in extreme weakness,
fluctuations in blood pressure, and chronic diarrhea and nausea,
among other symptoms. Kennedy also told the doctor about the
chronic and often acute back pain that had resulted from injuries
he had incurred while commanding a badly damaged and sinking
PT boat in the South Pacific in World War II. Kennedy, who had
suffered bone loss and was taking more than a few hot showers a
day as a kind of hydrotherapy, was almost crippled by the pain. He
wasn't wheelchair-bound, as Franklin Roosevelt had been after he
contracted polio, but he needed medication just to be able to walk
without crutches and to keep his pain at a low ebb. Dr. Janet Travell
was then treating Kennedy's back pain through a prescription of
injections of Procaine/Novocaine. This handicap, according to
Barbara Leaming, "was also difficult to hide from a public that
thought of him as athletic and robust. Something as simple as
bending over a lectern to read a speech caused him terrible pain.
Janet Travell worked with engineers to design a reading stand
that would reduce the pain."[8] However, Dr. Travell's specialty was
traditionally orthopedic. Jacobson was the miracle doctor Kennedy
needed to help him regain his energy.

Kennedy also revealed that he drank not an insubstantial amount of alcohol, partly because it went with a politician's territory of constantly having to attend social affairs. But he enjoyed drinking, too, Kennedy said. Jacobson was not a fan of alcohol himself and often weaned his patients off it. In Kennedy's case, it would prove to be an issue that his doctor would have to address constantly.

Kennedy was also very forthcoming about the prescription drugs he was taking. He was literally living in a chemical bath of medications. There was the Phenobarbital to control his irritable bowel syndrome; the cortisone steroids for his Addison's disease; the painkillers for his back; a series of sleeping aids; and antibiotics for various infections, including those of the urinary tract. He even took testosterone, which, combined with the effects of the methamphetamine, made Kennedy sexually ravenous. Although there was not much Jacobson could do about the Addison's disease, he assured Kennedy that his "vitamin cocktail" could help him manage the stress, extreme fatigue, and muscle weakness in preparation for the upcoming debates. After all, as Jacobson often told his patients, the treatment of stress was one of his specialties. Given Kennedy's medical condition, he knew the administration of a powerful stimulant might be dangerous, but at least it would give the young candidate enough energy to keep on facing the demands of the campaign head on. It was a risk Jacobson was willing to take. Not to worry, he told the candidate; he would be available to help Kennedy on a moment's notice. It would be his pleasure. Kennedy readily agreed to anything that would help him withstand the pain and give him back his strength. He didn't give a second thought about what was in the vial that Jacobson inserted into the needle of his syringe.

Dr. Jacobson's first injection took immediate effect as the methamphetamines hit his blood stream. Suddenly JFK, who had entered the office tired and weak, had a bounce in his step and could move more easily, despite the pain that he lived with every day of his adult life. He felt stronger, cool, focused, and very alert, he said. It was almost as if the patient had become another person, emerging like the mythical phoenix from the tired shell.

Others have described what Kennedy must have felt. Eddie Fisher said that after receiving the injection from Jacobson's inch-and-a-half needle, he felt as if he was being lit from within.[9] Truman Capote described it as "instant euphoria. You feel like Superman. You're flying. Ideas come at the speed of light. You go seventy-two hours straight without so much as a coffee break. You don't need sleep, you don't need nourishment. If it's sex you're after, you go all night. Then you crash—it's like falling down a well, like parachuting without a parachute. You want to hold onto something and there's nothing out there but air. You're going running back to East 72nd Street. You're looking for the German mosquito, the insect with the magic pinprick. He stings you, and all at once you're soaring again."[10]

So it was with John Kennedy. Jacobson gave him a bottle of "vitamin" drops—essentially another dose of methamphetamine—that he instructed him to take orally right before the debate with Nixon. That would fix him up, Jacobson said.

After his patient left, Jacobson felt more than satisfied that he had managed to affect symptomatic relief for the young senator. Jacobson already knew the long-term addictive effects of his injections. It only took one extraordinary high, followed by an equally extraordinary crash, and the patient would be back for more special elixir and would thereafter be under Jacobson's control. Control was the key, and Jacobson knew how to exert it.

While it could be said that Jacobson influenced the works of composer Leonard Bernstein, author Truman Capote, composer Alan Jay Lerner, and playwright Tennessee Williams with his magic potion, the doctor's crowning achievement occurred on the night of the first Nixon debate, where many have conjectured that the history of American politics changed. Nixon, who barely lost the popular vote in 1960 by just over 100,000 votes, was as powerful and aggressive a debater when it came to slugging it out as ever there was. Nixon extolled the virtues of a "rock 'em, sock 'em" campaign, bringing the fight directly to his opponent, whom he regarded as the enemy. As for Kennedy, although he had studied hard and tried to rest in preparation for the debate, he was hoarse and weak, his laryngitis had returned, and he was no match for the emboldened Richard Nixon, who was ahead in the polls.

On the evening of September 26, 1960, Kennedy visited Jacobson again, complaining in a voice barely above a whisper of extreme fatigue and lethargy. This time, Jacobson inserted his needle directly into Kennedy's throat and pumped methamphetamine into his voice box. The result was apparent in minutes. By the time Kennedy appeared on camera in his dark suit and professional make-up before an audience of seventy million television viewers, he seemed younger and far more vigorous than his opponent, the heavily perspiring vice president with the five o'clock shadow. Kennedy, who had been moribund, exhausted, and hoarse prior to the injection, was suddenly charismatic and radiated an energy that was contagious.

The difference between the candidates' appearances, their demeanors, and the way they responded to the questions made such an impression on the national viewing audience that in the polls, more than half of the voting public said they favored Kennedy's performance over Nixon's. Although Kennedy entered the debate behind Nixon, he emerged slightly ahead and gained the edge on that first night. That favorable initial impression was clearly important, because fewer people watched the ensuing debates. That first debate changed the outcome of the presidential campaign and, quite possibly, altered the course of modern American history.

That debate performance also put Max Jacobson at the top of JFK's medical priority list. JFK did not forget who and what had made him feel good. As Jacobson would record in his own notes, Kennedy had the ability to make someone feel as if that person were the most important person in the world. And for a refugee from Germany, the son of a kosher butcher who fled the Holocaust and struggled to gain a medical practice in New York in the late 1940s, Kennedy's bestowal of trust and friendship meant that he was accepted by the most powerful man on earth. It was a source of great pride.

Jacobson became a regular, if not constant, member of the Kennedy entourage. He responded to every summons from "Mrs. Dunn" and reinvigorated the president with his injections. After JFK won the election, he invited the Jacobsons to attend the inauguration and the balls that followed.

The Jacobsons were excited about attending the Kennedy inauguration, not just because of the honor it bestowed but because it also foretold a long and friendly relationship with JFK, a relationship that would put Jacobson in some of the most affluent and powerful circles in the world. He relished the opportunity and the power it conferred. Here he was treating the president of the United States by means of a potion that controlled the president's every emotion, his psychological state, and his physical capabilities.

For a control freak like Max Jacobson, this was the ultimate. Doris Shapiro, who was Allen Jay Lerner's assistant and one of Jacobson's patients, wrote, "Big Max, with his false savagery, thrived on dispensing his mythical powers."[11] Shapiro claimed that "Max was not a simple charlatan. He was a far more complicated one, brilliant, mysterious in his power to manipulate and orchestrate all the body systems and the mental ones, as well. He had about him a symptom of greatness. But he was corrupt to the core."[12] The most frightening part was that Max Jacobson now had control of the most powerful person in the world.

Inauguration Day, 1961. The morning was crisp and the air so cold that attendees could see the condensation from their breath freezing in the falling snow. The Jacobsons and their hosts, Senator Claude Pepper and his wife, were among the early arrivals and took their reserved seats about fifty yards from the presidential platform. Looking around at the shivering guests, Jacobson was concerned about the health and resilience of the president-elect. JFK had now become his personal president, and Jacobson extended his mantle of professional proprietorship over him. Jacobson peered at the crowd of dignitaries seated near the platform, picking out President Eisenhower, Vice President Nixon, and his soon-to-be patient, JFK's wife Jackie.

Despite the cold, and despite the crowd's amazement that the new president-elect who was about to be sworn in had removed his overcoat before the ceremony, everyone in attendance was wildly enthusiastic during Kennedy's inaugural address, a speech in which he laid out his agenda for a new generation of American leaders. Jacobson, who saw himself as key to Kennedy's victory because of his medical help, was especially proud of what his treatments had accomplished.

Due to the weather and Washington traffic, the Jacobsons and Peppers didn't reach the celebratory ball until close to midnight, where they met the legendary Joseph P. Kennedy and billionaire Cornelius Vanderbilt, Jr., shook the new president's hand, and watched Frank Sinatra perform in an astronaut costume. It was Jacobson's dream come true. And to think that it all started with a single injection to help Senator Kennedy overcome campaign stress and fatigue. Yes, Dr. Max Jacobson, who'd fled for his life from Nazi Berlin, had finally made it.

Despite the fact that he had been invited to the inaugural events, Jacobson was still surprised when he received a phone call from the White House prior to the president's trip to Canada in 1961. Dr. Janet Travell was on the other end, and she asked him detailed questions about his treatment of the president's stress. Travell explained that she needed to ensure Jacobson's treatment plan did not conflict with hers. Max explained how his treatments involved his special vitamin injections and how these injections relieved the president's fatigue.

Jacobson never shared the ingredients for his magic elixir with either colleagues or patients, even some of whom, such as Truman Capote, lived in fear that no other physician could duplicate the formula in case Jacobson was unavailable. Renowned New York psychiatrist Dr. Lawrence Hatterer once asked Jacobson for the ingredients of his formula to be able to treat his former patients now seeing Hatterer. Jacobson flatly replied, "I'll be glad to inject you with the drug so you can understand its effect." Hatterer promptly refused the offer.

Jacobson now tried the same tack with Travell and offered to send her the information in writing just in case she didn't get everything over the phone, as well as a sample of the fluid he was injecting. As psychiatrist Dr. Lawrence Hatterer would do the following year, Travell also refused to sample the drug and abruptly hung up. Jacobson later surmised that the real reason for Travell's call was that she realized he now had the president under his control. This control would come into play again at the upcoming Vienna Summit, where President Kennedy would soon face off with Premier Nikita Khrushchev of the Soviet Union at the height of the Cold War.

Chapter 2

A Kosher Butcher's Son

Who was the man who was now controlling with his addictive drugs an aspect of President Kennedy's behavior? Where did Dr. Max Jacobson come from, and how did he discover the concoction that would destroy so many lives?

"My father was a Kosher butcher," Dr. Max Jacobson often remarked whenever fortune bestowed its grace upon him. Leaving inaugural balls, meeting President Truman, waiting outside the meeting room in Vienna in case President Kennedy needed medical attention during his summit with Nikita Khrushchev, Jacobson would remind himself that although he might have been walking among the giants of his time, his origins were as humble as any could be. Controlled, as he was, by the drug that he was using to control others, Jacobson could remember a humbler time when only the world of scientific research was his Holy Grail. After all, Max didn't come from a powerful family. He came from a village where his family worked hard to survive.

Max Jacobson's family wasn't rich by any means. In fact, his hometown wasn't even a town. He was born in Fordon, a small village just inside the border of Poland on the banks of the Vistula River. Across the river was the warlike German state of Prussia. Fordon was almost like a shetl, one of the tiny villages out of stories of Sholem Aleicham in which the tiny Jewish community lived according to traditions and rules laid down 5,000 years earlier. In the town, young Max's father, Louis Jacobson, was the butcher. He had wanted to be a teacher, but he became a butcher so that he could pay his sisters' dowries; by the time he had raised the money to pay for them, he was forty years old—too old, he believed, to start an entirely new career. And so he remained a butcher and looked for a bride for himself.

Louis placed an announcement in the *Berliner Tageblatt* describing the type of woman he sought. As luck would have it, he found himself a match—Ernestine, a woman born in Heckelberg, a small village in Brandenburg consisting of about two hundred peasant families. Hers was the only Jewish family in the village, but her ancestors had lived in that village for two hundred years. She was descended from Moses Mendelsohn, a great philosopher at the court of King Frederick the Great of Prussia.

Ernestine had attended a girls' high school, where she learned secretarial skills and bookkeeping. After graduation, she moved in with a family living in Berlin and got a job in a small print shop. It was in that print shop that she came across Max's father's announcement. She responded to the ad, and they arranged to meet at a sweet shop. Jacobson later described his father's embarrassment when, unnerved by the woman's beauty, he plunked his top hat right into the whipped cream of her dessert. It was an auspicious introduction, which ultimately blossomed into a marriage for the man from a shetl in Poland.

The Jacobsons had three sons, of which Max, born on July 3, 1900, and named after his mother's brother, was the youngest. His Uncle Max had fought for Prussia, serving in the Guarde Kuirassier regiment, but had been wounded in the Franco-Prussian War and eventually died from his injuries. Max's Hebrew name was Moishe, after Moses Ben Maimonides, the great twelfth-century philosopher and physician. With three boys and a family business in a small village, things were tough for the Jacobsons. Ernestine finally came to the conclusion that they would be squeezed financially by the small returns from the butcher business and the overwhelmingly arduous work that Louis had to do.

Most kosher butchers bought their meat from the slaughterhouse. Max's father, however, because it was less expensive, had to buy live cattle, load the animals onto wagons himself, take them to the kosher slaughterer, and assist while the cattle were hoisted upside down on chains and killed by a single stroke. Then all the blood was drained out of the animals, in keeping with the commandment in the Torah that forbade the drinking of blood of any kind and in any form because "blood is the life thereof."

Ultimately, Louis conceded to his wife's wishes and moved the family to Berlin when Max was one year old. It was a fortuitous move because, in time, the little Polish village of Fordon would be occupied by the Nazis and the villagers forced at gunpoint to dig their own graves. They were then ordered to stand by the graves while Nazi gunners opened up, exterminating every villager and then closing the graves. This was the fate that the Jacobsons escaped.

The Jacobsons opened their new butcher shop on Magazin-strasse, one of the commercial thoroughfares in Berlin. They lived with Max's aunt and uncle along with three salesgirls and three butchers, all of whom worked in the business and had private apartments, more like small suites, in the building. In that house, Max decided at an early age that he would become a medical doctor. This, he said, was because of an accident that he had in his neighborhood along the Magazinstrasse.

Max described his neighborhood as a series of houses built around courtyards, separated from each other by tall, wrought-iron fences topped with sharp spikes. During the day, street merchants would enter the courtyards and call out, "Chairs to mend!" or "Knives to sharpen!" or whatever services they had to offer. Before the advent of shopping malls and centers, almost all of the commercial and retail activity was done in this manner, with many voices echoing off of many walls.

Max remembered the organ grinders in particular, along with other street musicians who traveled the neighborhoods. Children poked their heads out of windows in wonderment at the entertainment, and their parents, if they had the money, would throw coins into the courtyards. He was told that the coins people threw at them were the only way the street performers could manage to pay for their next meal. And those stories touched the young Max Jacobson. It was one of these very street performers, grinding away on his box organ while his costumed monkey danced for coins, who led to Max Jacobson's becoming a medical doctor.

One day an organ grinder came into the Jacobsons' part of the courtyard with his monkey, both dressed in shabby clothes. The people living above the courtyard, as was their custom, threw open their windows and tossed coins into the yard. As he looked out the window, young Max could see that some of the coins had landed on the other side of the fence. This was a chance for Max to perform a *mitzvah,* an act of pure altruism for no other purpose than to help someone else, which was a form of *tzadikah,* or righteousness, the definition of a good deed. Max tried to retrieve the coins for the organ grinder by climbing over the courtyard fence, but as he did, he impaled himself on one of the spikes. The shock was so sudden and intense that Max only vaguely noticed any pain, but he could feel the blood running down his leg. He managed to disengage himself by pulling himself across the spike, which only made the gash worse. When he ran into the house, his mother took one look at his face and knew something was terribly wrong. Fearing he would get into trouble for climbing over the fence, Max denied anything was wrong, but there was the blood to prove it. His mother called the family doctor.

Beloved by all the village, the village doctor was a middle-aged man with a big black mustache, who was always chewing on a cigar, even when it wasn't lit. He always arrived in a horse-drawn coach driven by a uniformed coachman wearing large boots and a top hat. And when the doctor examined his patients, he would first place his cigar in a small metal etui—a small decorative box designed to hold personal items—which he would place on the window sill so that the smoke would vent outside. He was a compassionate and understanding man, Max remembered, and embodied qualities that were reassuring to a patient. All of this clearly made an impression on young Max.

As Max stood at the window waiting for the doctor's arrival, the doctor returned Mrs. Jacobson's call, telling her that Max's wound would most likely require suturing and that his son-in-law should handle the case because he was a surgeon. When the surgeon arrived in a shiny new 1905 automobile wearing a cap, goggles, and a big duster, the sight was so thrilling that Max completely forgot about his wound. The surgeon removed his gloves, duster, and jacket, washed his hands, and positioned Max across the arms of a stuffed chair to give him unobstructed access to the wound. First, the surgeon stuck an iodine-drenched piece of cotton into the wound to disinfect it. Then, without any anesthesia, he threw suture after suture through the torn skin to close it. He covered the sutures with adhesive and gauze and promised to return to look over the stitches. By the time he returned to remove them, Max's heart was set on becoming a doctor so that he, too, could drive such a magnificent automobile.

Mrs. Jacobson was determined that, in spite of the expense, her sons would receive the benefits of higher education. She enrolled her children in the Koenigstadtische Real Gymnasium, which covered elementary school, junior high, and high school. At the end of the ninth year, an examination called *das eingaerige* ("the one-year") was administered to students entering their sophomore year of high school. Those who passed the test earned the privilege of one year of military service rather than the compulsory three years. At the end of his twelfth year, a successful graduate received the Abiturium, a kind of automatic college acceptance, to enroll in university.

Max was a good student who studied hard and was fascinated by medicine and science. When he was eleven years old, his parents gave him a microscope as a present. He often went with his father to the slaughterhouse to obtain specimens for his microscopic observation. He discovered the structure of tissue cells, examined the nature of cow's blood, and taught himself how to prepare slides. What Max learned on his own was stimulated by the physics, chemistry, and zoology courses he took in school. He was also enrolled in a boys club, much like today's Boy Scouts, through which he had more opportunities to study nature.

Like many young Germans at the outbreak of World War I, Max, now fourteen, was loyal and patriotic. German Jews as well as Gentiles supported their Kaiser, who marched them off to war. Max watched as the older boys took their school exams so that they could volunteer for the army and be rushed to the front. Max remembered how his older friends made the quick transition from school clothing to army uniforms, took what today would be called "army basic training," and then marched in formation to the music of a military band. The early successes of the Kaiser's army made for heady news on the home front, with stories of the German invasion of Belgium and France and victory in Russia; however, this was not a nineteenth-century Prussian war. The modern weapons, such as machine guns and large artillery, were so destructive that soon Germans were reminded of the toll of war when news of the deaths of their friends and relatives made its way back home. The German economy began to strain and then buckle under the burden of war. Shortages became obvious when food stamps were issued and rationing began.

People stood in long lines to receive bare necessities, and in 1917, when Max's brothers were already at the Italian Front in the Signal Corps, the only food that was readily available was turnips. People found them in bakery shops disguised as cakes and bread. Potatoes were luxuries, as were milk and butter. People who could afford it obtained heavily rationed items through the black market, but amid the wartime controls, both the seller and the buyer became liable to the risk of severe penalties. And public health was also an issue because black market meats were not inspected and raised the risk of trichinosis and other diseases.

In 1917, when he was seventeen, Max graduated from Real Gymnasium, and was looking at the reality of being drafted into the army and sent to the trenches on the Western Front when he turned eighteen. Friends urged him to enlist as a library assistant at the front, which would preclude him from being drafted and land him a noncombat position, at least for the duration of the war. As he weighed this option, Max also had to deal with the news that both his older brothers, Heinz and Simon, had become war casualties—Heinz from a case of dysentery and Simon from shrapnel wounds.

Max broached the idea of enlisting as a library assistant to his parents, but they rejected it out of hand. He was still seventeen and not yet an adult. However, his mother had an idea. She called Dr. Adler, her surgeon, who was the head of Pankow Hospital just outside of Berlin, and asked him if there was any position open for Max at the hospital. She told him that Max wanted to become a doctor and that serving as a medical assistant, especially during wartime, might further that aim. Dr. Adler said there was a great shortage of medical personnel and arranged an interview for Max.

Working at the hospital was a revelation for Max. He got the job on the spot, working for Dr. Adler's assistant surgeon and son-in-law, Dr. Lutz, and was assigned to clean instruments and disinfect the operating room. Max was even permitted to be among the attendants at operations and autopsies. It was a way for Max to learn basic anatomy and medical procedures, almost as if he were already a second- or third-year medical student. He even accompanied the doctors during their rounds, and he learned to take blood pressure and pulse, administer injections, and change wound dressings. Not only was Max exposed to the practice of medicine;

he was also performing the duties of a hospital nurse.

The lack of antibiotics in those days resulted in rampant infections in the surgical hospitals. For example, if an inflammation was discovered in the thin tissue of the inner lining of a patient's (the peritoneum), during a basic abdominal surgery, there was little a surgeon could do to prevent peritonitis, a progressively painful condition that resulted not only from the wound itself but also from infection entering the wound. Max said that this was an all-too-common condition because of the filthy conditions on the battlefield and the time it took to move wounded soldiers from the front to the hospital. Surgeons could remove the bullets or shrapnel, but the inflammation and infection were usually the killers. As a result, the ironic expression, in those days as it is today, was "the operation went well, but the patient died."

The Pankow Hospital, like other surgical facilities across Germany, was inundated with war wounded and had transformed its specialty facilities to handle the triage and treatment of casualties. Max remembered that a wing of the hospital, which had been isolated because it was used for tuberculosis patients, was now transformed into a military hospital for the most severely injured soldiers. Drs. Adler and Lutz were the only surgeons in the hospital at that time and were required to treat both military as well as civilian patients. Because of the shortage of medical personnel, Dr. Adler's own wife served as the operating room nurse, even while Dr. Adler himself had to cover the surgical service at two other Berlin hospitals.

Max described the conditions at his hospital as adverse at best and fatally critical at worse. *Infectious austeomyelitis*, an infection of the bone, often lingered in patients for many years. It was an infection brought about, during wartime, by the septic nature of bullets and shrapnel. It was difficult to treat before the development of antibiotics and severely weakened a patient's entire immune system. Gangrene, always a problem in wartime because of the septic nature of wounds, often progressed faster than the amputations performed to arrest it. Moreover, because neither the means to prevent tetanus nor the means to treat it had been discovered, doctors had to stand by while patients died, their bodies wracked with cramps and their death masks a testament to the pain they endured as infection ravaged their bodies. Max would attend the two doctors and their nurses when they removed blood-drenched bandages applied at the front to soldiers' wounds. Max saw how the wounds were literally infested with crawling maggots. It was a gruesome sight, but it wasn't until years later that doctors discovered what indigenous and native populations already knew: Flesh-eating larvae cleansed the wound of decaying tissue. And Max watched all this and learned.

The Spanish flu pandemic in 1917 brought more chaos to a hospital already overwhelmed by the casualties of war. Max said that doctors watched helplessly as victims died within twenty-four hours of contracting the disease and were as horrified at the speed of the epidemic's spread as they were at the speed of the acceleration of the patients' symptoms. The bluish-black discoloration of the victims' faces, resulting from a loss of oxygen as the flu filled up their lungs and brought on congestive heart failure, resembled that caused by the Black Death of the Middle Ages. Hospital beds were already filled up by wounded soldiers, and hospitals could not stretch their services or even provide beds for the flu victims. Morgues, too, were overwhelmed as the city faced the problem of providing for the families of the dead. But through it all, though the cause of the disease was unknown and there were no preventive measures or therapies for the patients, the flu did not strike the hospital staff in any great numbers. Max was among the lucky who never contracted the flu.

Max had a rude introduction to the social and moral deterioration of Germany when he first encountered victims of the "hunger riots." He was heading home after working the night shift at the hospital when the tramway car he was riding stopped because of a street disturbance. Max saw three men beating two women; he left the train and rushed to their defense. But the men quickly overpowered Max, leaving him half-conscious on the street. He was handcuffed and taken to police headquarters, where he was thrown into a jail cell. As he was dragged to the cell, police officers left their desks to kick and beat him. He was then tossed into a cell containing other battered individuals, indigents, and drunks who were barely conscious.

Max heard about the hunger riots from the other prisoners. The two women Max had tried to protect were protestors in those riots and had been set on by the police. The riots had begun with the mutiny of a group of sailors in Kiel, the main base of the German Navy on the North Sea. Sailors were protesting conditions in the navy, lack of pay, and shortages of food. The mutiny was put down by the military, and the crown clamped down on the story, censuring news reports of the mutiny. But despite the censure, word of the rebellion spread across Germany and inspired the hunger riots. Germany was seething under the burden of war, war that was draining the civilian population of its resources and placing burdens on all of the public health systems. Max was among the lucky, however, because even though he had been beaten and thrown into jail, one of his father's clients was the desk sergeant taking roll call of the jailed prisoners. He recognized Max, heard his story of how he ran afoul of the police, and released him from prison.

Max turned eighteen the following year and received his draft notice for the 65th Field Artillery Regiment in Deutsch-Aylau, a small city near the Russian Frontier. The war had been ravaging Europe for long enough that the populations in both Germany and in Russia were disaffected with their imperial leaders and disenchanted with any glory based on victory in war. As Max remembered it, Germany was demoralized, and the government was near collapse. Kaiser Wilhelm, who'd led the nation into war with Russia, Great Britain, and France, had fled to Holland as social unrest swept the country. In his place, the Germans had installed the Weimar Republic, a social democratic movement. For Max, this meant that by the time his basic army training was to have been completed, Germany would have already been defeated. But the war was still on, and Max still had to report to his draft board.

Max's mother did not want her son to go to the front. She had already lost one son to war. How ironic would it be, as all of Germany gradually collapsed and submitted to a bitter peace, for her son to be one of the final casualties of the war? She vowed she would not let this happen. Through the grapevine, Mrs. Jacobson heard that the district draft board director, a retired military officer of great stature and even greater pomposity, had an obsession for the nearly unobtainable Liederkranz cheese, so precious in ration-driven Germany that finding it was like finding gold. Max's mother, the wife of a butcher who knew where items could be found at a price, managed to bargain for a piece of Liederkranz, wrapped and boxed it, and sent Max off to his local draft board with, as he described it, a big wooden box under his arm.

The rumors about the draft board director of Max's district were true. He was a crotchety old man, hobbled by wounds from prior wars, limping around his office and weighed down by a long cavalry saber that dragged across the floor. Under his bald crown, he stared hard at Max, a stare made even more menacing by the man's thick walrus moustache. Max remembered that moustache challenging him as he entered the director's office, a moustache that began to quiver ever so slightly as the director sniffed the air. Then he focused his glare at the box tucked under Max's arm.

His hard glare seemed to melt as he looked at the box. "And what can I do for you, young man?" he said.

"I'm Max Jacobson," Max said, announcing himself and continuing that he was following his orders to report for induction.

"Very commendable," the director said, staring longingly at the box under Max's arm. He walked around the desk toward Max. "The Kaiser needs every man he can get at the Polish Front."

Max began his pitch. Though he had received his induction notice, he already had two brothers serving in the army, both of whom had suffered casualties. Max was the sole son left at home. Max also said that he was working at the Pankow Hospital in Berlin, serving as a medical assistant in surgery. The shortage in medical personnel was acute, Max explained, which was why his duties in the operating room dealing with wounded combat veterans was so important. He would soon be entering medical school, Max said. And then he put the box of cheese right on the director's desk.

The district draft board director stared directly at the box on the desk, his moustache twitching as the aroma of cheese permeated the room. Then he said, "Well, what's one man more or less at the Polish Front?" And Max left the office. He was not inducted.

Max enrolled as a pre-med at the Fredrich Wilhelm University in Berlin, where his first class was human anatomy, and was quickly overwhelmed by the huge volume of reading his professor piled on his desk. In fact, the stack of books was so tall that it obscured the tiny professor who was sitting behind it. Max later remembered that he believed he was staring into the face of failure and feared even more that he would have to confess to his mother that he was just not up to the task.

But as he sat in the lecture hall and looked around him, he saw that many of the students in his class were just very young soldiers, almost all of whom were officers, only recently returned from the front and discharged from military service. They were dressed in shabby uniforms, and many had been wounded and were on crutches. Max also noticed that the officers had removed their insignias, probably to avoid being killed by their own men as they retreated from the front. Things at the front were that bad. As he looked over his competition, Max's confidence returned. He told himself that if others in his class could do it, so could he. And he did. He passed his anatomy course within the year, and when he was nineteen, he transferred to Albert Ludwigs-Universitat in Freiburg, one of the oldest universities in Germany. It was at Freiburg that Max attended the lectures of Professor Wilhelm C. Roentgen, the developer of X-ray photography. Max had worked with X-ray technology at the hospital in Pankow where it was used, as it is today, for diagnostic evaluation.

X-ray technology had opened up an entirely new window into the study of anatomy. Instead of looking at detailed drawings or examining the internal organs of cadavers, X-rays allowed young medical students to see the actual process of the functioning body. By having patients or subjects swallow a substance called barium sulfate, a metallic substance that illuminates the digestive tract, doctors could use X-rays to see if there were any abnormalities in the soft tissue. Barium X-rays were used by gastroenterologists. Max remembered how he liked to see the X-ray machine come to life when the switch was thrown. He would marvel at the way the bare copper wires connecting the vacuum tube to the transformer began sparkling in the dark with a crackling sound. Then Max would watch the fluorescent screen in fascination as the barium paste traveled down the esophagus, through the stomach, and into the intestinal tract. Barium illuminated the soft tissue in the chest cavity, bedazzling the students who watched the rising and falling of the diaphragm during respiration, the mechanism of joints in use, and the simultaneous peristalsis of the intestines. Through the lectures at Freiburg, Max acquired an understanding of the nature of the X-rays and saw how Roentgen opened a new field of radiology in medicine. And after his studies in Freiburg, Max returned to Berlin to continue his medical study.

Max had returned to a different Berlin, a city no longer peaceful in a country wracked by the terms of the treaty of Versailles. The economy was in ruins, the Army was now a local police force, and the old generals who had lost the Kaiser's war were organizing a fifth column called the Black Army. The generals claimed that leftists had become the enemy that destroyed the empire, and by 1919, there were street fights between the forces of the Weimar Republic and the Schwarzer Reichswehr, the Black Army.

The right wing claimed that the leftists were liberals stabbing the military in the back. Social democrats, the Black Army claimed, were little better than the communists who undermined the structure of the country's moral fiber. Public demonstrations turned into violent confrontations and to open fighting in the streets. During one of the street fights, Max took shelter in a recessed entrance to a building. As the fighting raged outside, Max looked around to find that someone was also taking shelter in the doorway. Max introduced himself, and the gentleman extended his hand and said that his name was Albert Einstein. Max knew who he was, of course. The two men shared their fears about the country, but Einstein had only one fear, he said: "Only that I wouldn't be able to find things on my desk after my maid had tidied it up."

In 1920, Max transferred to the University of Wurzburg to continue his studies. Wurzburg was still a medieval city housing a great university where Max, refusing to join one of the dueling fraternities that still practiced the illegal sport, became the surgeon in training, repairing the physical injuries to the duelists. And after that year, Max returned to Berlin, where he became a "candidate of medicine," meaning he passed his basic exams in anatomy, physics, chemistry, and physiology and was set to advance to attending lectures at the city's teaching hospitals. There he studied internal medicine, gynecology, obstetrics, surgery, and pathology at lectures in auditoriums where the instructors demonstrated everything from diagnoses to operations and post-operative care. Max and his fellow students also followed hospital rounds and served as interns in outpatient clinics, where they learned the actual practice of general medicine.

Amidst the changing cultural milieu of the 1920s, medicine, Max noticed, was still an art at the turn of the century. Doctors had to rely on their own sensory impressions of patient presentations and the symptoms doctors could see for themselves. Radiology and laboratory tests, the lynchpins of today's medicine, were not always readily available, even in Berlin, and very often beyond the means of the average patients. And given the sometimes difficult task of differentiating between diseases presenting similar symptoms, Max learned the art of diagnosis. It would be a skill that he would boast about and would stay with him throughout his career.

Max considered himself a scientist as well as a healer. He experimented with new medicines, particularly for the treatment of diabetics. Max learned that it was not only his stethoscope that was an essential tool, but also his ability to listen to a patient describe symptoms, the tone of a patient's voice, and even his choice of words. As successful as he was as a diagnostician, he, too, was among those doctors who stood helplessly by as infectious diseases ran their course and took a toll on the population.

Max's interests centered around biochemistry, the subject of his doctoral dissertation and one of the core elements of his practice. Max was fascinated by development of new medications, a route opened up for him by his interest in biochemistry. He was so fascinated by the research into new drugs that he and his fellow doctoral students often tried out the new medications on themselves. They believed it was the best method of familiarizing themselves with the new drugs and their effects, as well as their side effects. When he tested a substance called nicotinic acid, a member of the B-complex vitamin group, to see whether it would enhance his feeling of well-being, Max suffered a painful reaction so severe that he thought he would die. However, because the effects almost immediately subsided, he was not dissuaded from self-testing.

Max's next internship was at the Surgical University Clinic of the College of Sports and Gymnastics working under Professor Auguste Bier, a man in his early sixties, who sported a large, white moustache and spoke in a deep voice that always sounded patronizing to his patients and students. Dr. Bier, in Max's words, was a combination of surgeon and homeopathic physician. Dr. Bier's theory of injecting patients with small doses of infectious bacteria so as to trigger the formation of antibodies specific to fight that bacteria became the basis for the modern medical procedure of inoculation. The theory behind vaccinations and immunizations today stems, in part, from Dr. Bier's theory of immunization. Bier used this same theory to experiment with controlling the infections from meningitis as well as from endocarditis, an infection of the heart muscle. Endocarditis, in the 1920s, had a 100 percent mortality rate. But Dr. Bier's treatment of burning the skin above the infection to increase the body's resistance to the infection did not work, and Bier's experimental treatment ended in failure.

In addition to surgical procedures, Bier experimented with creating antibiotics, skin grafting, spinal fusion, and other techniques that required an understanding of cellular composition. His methods were questioned by his peers in the medical community primarily because they were quite controversial at the time. Jacobson recalled that Bier was always looking for new therapies to remedy various disorders. Bier had grown up in a farming community, what Jacobson referred to as "peasant stock," and observed in detail how nature could provide him with clues he could apply to medicine.[13]

According to Jacobson, Bier was also a free thinker, who respected the work of scientists and microanalyses, the study of molecules and chemical structures. Despite the advances made in science and medicine during the mid-nineteenth to early twentieth century, Bier remarked that he had greater admiration for his dog because just by sniffing a lamppost, it could tell whether a friend or foe had been there.[14]

Under Bier, Jacobson refined his already sharp skills as a diagnostician, explaining that

I learned the danger of a physician's jumping to an obvious diagnosis that was impressed on me indelibly by an emergency case that had been admitted after an accident. The patient was brought to the auditorium where an intern proudly diagnosed a broken clavicle. Professor Bier walked over and reexamined the patient. "Sir," he said, "this is a splendid diagnosis and a good presentation. There is only one thing you overlooked. This man also has a busted spleen." He then turned to the class and said: "Gentlemen, you may be very satisfied when you discover something on which you can hang your diagnosis. But don't stop there. Remember, a human being, too, can have both lice and fleas."[15]

As Jacobson pursued his medical internship with Bier, he was very aware of the deterioration in the German economy. Terrible inflation had set in, causing great unrest in the population. Jacobson's father, for example, complained to him that prices were rising so fast that no matter how much he sold a steak for, he had to pay more for meat from his supplier at the slaughterhouse.

Jacobson, too, needed to find a way to finance his studies. He took a job trading stocks by telephone at the Berlin Stock Exchange, where he discovered, to his happiness, that his knowledge of math enabled him to make quick currency conversion calculations for currency trades. Thus, Jacobson began to succeed as a day trader even as he helped support his family's failing business and his own medical studies.

In 1929, Jacobson graduated from medical school. The only thing he needed to complete his requirements for a medical license was his final internship, which he took at the Charité University Hospital. His surgery internship was at the Surgical University Clinic, where he had worked under Dr. Bier, and where he had learned how biological cells operate, reproduce and can be regenerated.

Jacobson, while on a vacation from his internship at the surgical hospital, made a short trip to Marienbad to join his parents, who were staying at the health spa, bathing in the natural springs, and simply taking a break from the economic worries afflicting most of Germany, particularly Berlin. It was at Marienbad where Jacobson met a quiet and studious young woman named Alice Lowner. The two hit it off and became engaged. The couple decided to get married after Jacobson received his medical degree, which he did. He then became a general practitioner with his own office while volunteering as a surgical assistant to Dr. Bier.

With a new wife and a newly minted medical degree, with a new office as a general practitioner, and with what he hoped was a bright future before him, Dr. Max Jacobson thus began the third phase of his young life as a professional physician in Berlin.

Chapter 3

Setting Up Shop in Berlin

Max Jacobson and his new bride, Alice Lowner, set up their first apartment in a fashionable part of Berlin near a park surrounding the Chateau Belle Vue. Jacobson also opened his private practice while he continued to work as a member of a medical research team at the Charité Hospital, where he investigated the changes in blood chemistry. He worked with doctors who, in addition to experimenting on animals, also experimented on themselves to obtain insight as to the effects of new drugs, a practice that Jacobson would also adopt, which ultimately got him addicted to methamphetamines. Jacobson also tried to develop a clientele of patients across the range of economic classes. He had wealthy patients as well as humble ones from working-class backgrounds. But as much as his fascination was with his general practice, he also developed an interest in the new field of psychiatry. He made the acquaintance of the three greatest psychiatrists of the time: Sigmund Freud, Carl Jung, and Alfred Adler. Max met Freud, who was suffering from a cancer of his tongue. Mouth, tongue, throat, and esophageal cancers are among the types of cancers usually associated with heavy cigar and pipe smoking. Although Freud had become famous all across the world by the 1920s, his life had been plagued by financial problems. Despite those, his research flourished. Early on in his studies of brain anatomy, he discovered the cerebral location that caused speech disturbance in children. He was one of the early researchers on the biology of the brain that demystified the operation of the human neurological system at a time well before modern brain imaging studies. He faced great resistance from the medical profession when he articulated his concept of psychoanalysis. There was much derision from his colleagues when Freud presented his ideas about the unconscious mind, the influence of the human sex drive on the development of personality, and the methods a doctor should use in trying to ascertain the root causes of psychological disturbances. Most people believe, Max once said, that for Freud, psychoanalysis was an end in itself. But that was not true. Freud believed that medical research would ultimately reveal the biological workings of the brain and would result in the development of medications that would treat pathological mental illness.

Max also consulted on cases with Professor Carl Jung. In one particular instance, a wealthy patient suffering from a neurosis had contacted Max for help. Max contacted Jung, and the two talked not only about the case, but also at length about Jung's theory of the collective unconscious and the archetypal symbols of human beliefs. It was while studying under these psychiatrists that Jacobson began to experiment with methamphetamines as mood enhancers and emotional stimulants and applied his skills in the science of organic and biochemistry to the study of psychology. His research under the tutelage of Carl Jung led him to first experiment with early psychotropic, or mood and mind-altering, drugs that would by the latter part of the twentieth century result in pharmaceuticals such as Paxil, Ritalin, and even LSD. Jacobson noted that Jung himself foresaw the development of drugs that would normalize aberrant brain behavior. Jacobson looked for ways he could mix these early mind-altering drugs with vitamins, enzymes, animal placentas, and small amounts of hormones to remedy illnesses stemming from malnutrition or the abuse of alcohol or drugs such as tranquilizers.[16] Jacobson experimented on animals, patients, and himself with these drug cocktails. He became fascinated with the effects of the drugs he concocted and came to believe he could effect remedies on a cellular level through his own types of biological elixirs.

Max's internship and assistantship in surgery with August Bier, though it introduced him to the basics of surgical procedures, nevertheless convinced him that what he really wanted to practice was internal medicine. He said that he believed he could bring about more healing that way. Surgery in the 1920s was quite dangerous because of the side effects of anesthesia and the risk of infection. Infection was so insidious that despite the best efforts of hospital operating rooms to maintain sanitary conditions, infections were rampant and difficult to prevent or control. Surgery, although preferred as a specialty by many new physicians in Europe, was limited by the conditions at hospitals. Therefore, Max Jacobson, who was fascinated by the body's own biological chemistry, decided that his specialty would be internal medicine. Following the education he received at the feet of his first mentor, Dr. Bier, Jacobson began his own practice at the Charité University Hospital in Berlin, which is still one of the largest hospitals in the world. He assembled a specially designed laboratory in his private office, where his experiments included an investigation into the changes in blood chemistry through the use of choline, the basic component for the neurotransmitter acetylcholine; Belafoline, a drug used in the treatment of migraines or severe headaches; and ergotomin (or gynergen), a blood constrictor also used to alleviate pain. Jacobson published his scientific study of gynergen and its use in gynecology and migraines, and in the treatment of the confusion caused by cerebral sclerosis. He also continued his lifelong practice of testing drugs on himself, because he admired doctors who did so to learn their side effects.[17]

Because Germany was still dealing with soldiers who'd lost limbs and whose internal organs were deteriorating from diseases they'd contracted at the front, doctors by the late 1920s were researching the methods of transplanting organs—and particularly the rejection of transplants. Skin transplants were also an issue because so many soldiers had suffered from disfiguring burns and burns that had become infected. Doctors also looked for ways to remove scar tissue without re-infecting a wound. Max was one of the early experimenters, using the blood serum from animals to prevent immune rejection to hetero-skin transplants. He injected guinea pigs with extracts of skin and feathers. He found that he was able to keep skin transplants for as much as one-third of the animal's surface in place for months at a time. The chemicals from feathers and skin helped destroy the toxins in cells and formed the basis of Max's later experiments with treating malignant growths that developed into tumors. Max believed that his concoctions of animal blood serum enabled him to control the symptoms of high blood pressure as well as detoxification of infections. Based on this research, Max thought he had found a way to remediate the symptoms of some types of neurosis as he experimented with the physiological basis of mental illness. These experiments, particularly experiments in refining animal blood serum and combining it with pharmaceuticals to be injected intravenously, would ultimately become the basis for Max's injections of liquid methamphetamines mixed with goat's and sheep's blood for boosting his patient's abilities to withstand stress and rise above the difficulties in their lives. In other words, Max was looking for ways to get his patients high enough to slough off whatever was troubling them, even if what was troubling them were progressive diseases that could not be cured.

Deciding to become an internist rather than a surgeon at Charité University Hospital, Jacobson began more intensely studying the effects of his methamphetamine mixtures on both himself and his patients. He worked in the laboratories at Charité to create his own special formula that would allow his patients to "feel good." But as Dr. Leslie Iversen, the author of *Speed, Ecstasy, Ritalin: The Science of Amphetamines*,[4] points out, Jacobson's "mistake was testing the drug on himself. It distorts the senses and does not allow for a scientist to empirically study the drug."

Jacobson focused his research on amphetamine, a drug that has been in circulation in various forms and compounds for more than one hundred years, and which is still prescribed today to treat Attention Deficit Disorder (ADD) or Attention Deficit Hyperactivity Disorder (ADHD). Some say the powerful amphetamine formula that is supposed to remedy these disorders is a wonder drug. Others call it a gateway drug. Either way, it can be harmful if not monitored, but it is far less harmful than its sister drug, methamphetamine, which is a psycho-stimulant drug. Because its molecules are similar in shape and size to the neurotransmitter dopamine, the pleasure-sensing neurotransmitter, it can fool the brain's neurons into treating its presence just like dopamine. Dopamine tells the cells of the brain to feel pleasure and even euphoria. The more dopamine that's transmitted from brain cell to brain cell, the greater and longer-lasting the pleasure high. Simply stated, methamphet-amines make you feel good—really good. However, that feeling can often be followed by severe manic-depression, paranoid delusions of hypergrandiosity, schizophrenic dissociative behavior, and at its worst, a complete breakdown of logical perception. Methamphet-amine can also cause a rise in the user's blood pressure, an increased heart rate, and even a heart attack. And this is not to mention that methamphetamine is also highly addictive.

Methamphetamine was first synthesized by a Japanese scientist in 1919 and used by the Germans as well as the British in World War II. During the 1920s it was widely considered a wonder drug and was used to treat everything from asthma to nasal congestion. While amphetamines had been first approved to be sold in tab-let form by the American Medical Association in 1937, metham-phetamine had been first marketed over the counter as an inhaler known as Benzedrine by the drug manufacturer Smith, Kline, and French beginning in 1932. By 1940, physicians treating their pa-tients for narcolepsy and ADHD with the tablet form that was marketed over the counter by manufacturer Burroughs Wellcome, who called it Methedrine. Widely prescribed in America and abroad in the 1950s, meth was used to treat everything from alcoholism (by simply transferring the addiction mechanism) to Parkinson's disease.

Throughout Berlin, word spread about Jacobson's successful treatment of some of the symptoms of Multiple Sclerosis (MS) and the tremendous boost of energy that his injections created in his patients. He attracted, as he would later in his Manhattan practice, various well-known German musicians and theater people, includ-ing the Austrian-born filmmaker Billy Wilder.[18] In her worldwide best-seller *Around the World in Eleven Years*, published in 1936, American author Patience Abbe recalled meeting Dr. Max in Berlin when she was ten years old: "I had contracted the mumps and needed the assistance of a physician. We were sent to a wonderful physician named Doctor Max Jacobson. Doctor Jacobson was a magician. He put a piece of clay in my ear and it came out of my head. He was an acrobat, magician, and a Doctor and he loved us."[19] Jacobson had performed a magic trick to gain the confidence of his young patient.

The growing notoriety of Jacobson's vitamin cocktail attracted the attention of the National Socialists, and they demanded to know the formula concocted by this Jewish doctor. Before he escaped with his family—first to Czechoslovakia and then to Vienna, Paris, and the United States—Jacobson handed over the formula, which he claimed was used by the German army. He believed that the Nazis handed his formula to the pharmaceutical company Temmler, which then manufactured the drug under the name Pervitin.[20] Pervitin was in fact a methamphetamine drug introduced into the market in 1938 and was what propelled the Wehrmacht soldiers through much of the Blitzkrieg.

The German military was supplied with millions of methamphetamine tablets during the first half of 1940. The drugs were part of a plan to help pilots, sailors, and infantry troops become capable of sustained and even superhuman performance. The military leadership liberally dispensed such stimulants, as long as it believed drugging the troops could help achieve victory over the Allies. But the Nazis were less than diligent in monitoring side effects such as drug addiction, depression, violence, and a consequent decline in moral standards.[21]

During the short period between April and July 1940, more than thirty-five million tablets of Pervitin and Isophan, a slightly modified version produced by the Knoll pharmaceutical company, would be shipped to the German army and Luftwaffe.[22] Some of the tablets, each containing three milligrams of active substance, were sent to the Wehrmacht's medical divisions under the code name OBM, and then distributed directly to the troops. A rush order could even be placed by telephone if a shipment was urgently needed. The packages were labeled STIMULANT, and the instructions recommended a dose of one to two tablets "only as needed, to maintain sleeplessness."[23] Jacobson strongly believed that both Hitler and his mistress Eva Braun were addicted to the methamphetamine formula he had created in its liquid, injected form, according to Dr. Bert E, Park in *Aging, Ailingt, and Addicted.*[5]

As Max's practice flourished, he was soon the go-to doctor for all sorts of emergencies. He treated the former Kaiser's son, who suffered a fall from a horse, and also treated a young woman named Nina Hagan whose foot was almost crushed by a horse. Max found an orthopedic surgeon, a friend of his wife, who performed a successful operation that restored the use of Ms. Hagan's foot. Little did Max know at the time, he once said, that this young patient would ultimately become his next wife.

By 1932, life was gradually, but very perceptibly, becoming more and more dangerous for the Jewish population of Germany, particularly in Berlin. Max described to friends after he arrived in the United States that the Brown Shirts began roaming the streets of Berlin and assaulting anyone who looked Jewish. Not only were there taunts and threats, but Jews were also beaten severely. Jews were pushed off the streets when the Brown Shirts marched, singing the song "Juden Blut vom Messer spritzt" (Jewish blood drips from our knives). And then Hitler's followers started the fire in the

Reichstag, the government building, thus bringing about "kristallnacht" or the "night of the broken glass," when mobs, blaming the Jews for the fire, destroyed Jewish-owned shops and homes. The Reichstag fire brought about Hitler's rise to power and the enactment of the Nuremberg laws.

One late afternoon in 1932, a Brown Shirt knocked furiously on Max's door. Max told the young man that because he was a Jewish doctor, he was not allowed to see or treat him. But the man pushed his way into the office and whispered that he couldn't talk to an Aryan physician because he had contracted gonorrhea. This impurity was forbidden in the ranks of the Brown Shirts and would have meant the man's expulsion and punishment. Hence, his only choice was to talk to a Jewish doctor, also a forbidden act in Nazi Germany.

Max treated him and then heard the terrible information. "I am grateful to you," the Brown Shirt said, looking menacingly at the doctor. "Here is how I'll prove my gratitude. Your life is in acute danger. You are on the list of our 'Roll Kommando." Roll Kommando was a special unit of the Brown Shirt secret police, almost like an assassination unit, formed to eliminate those whom the Reich deemed "undesirables." Jewish professionals or prominent Jews were high on the list. Max got the message: Get out fast. Max and Alice and their very young son, Thomas, fled from Berlin the very next day, heading for Prague and the home of Alice's parents. Max was fortunate to have pulled up stakes so quickly, because the day after he left Germany, his nurse, a woman who had worked for him for many years, was arrested, and Max had to hire a Nazi lawyer to get her freed. Max had begun the next phase of his life, an émigré fleeing that would, in just a few years, become the Holocaust and the extermination of six million of Europe's Jewish population.

Chapter 4

A New Life in Czechoslovakia and Paris

"Decisions are simple when there are no alternatives."

—Dr. Max Jacobson

Jacobson might have felt an immediate respite from danger when he, his wife, and his child crossed the frontier into Czechoslovakia, but that respite didn't last for long. Nor did the feeling of freedom because, after recovering from the disorientation and shock at immigration, Jacobson believed that he had no hope of reestablishing his medical practice in Prague. He'd left everything behind in Berlin: his possessions, his equipment, his medicines, and his instruments. Moreover, he believed (and history would prove him right) that there was the threat of imminent invasion and occupation by the Nazis, making any permanent settlement in Prague a danger. After all, when the Nazis came to power, their first targets were the Jews. And among the Jews, the professionals, particularly the high-profile professionals, were viewed as undesirables.

At first, the Jacobsons moved in with Alice's parents, but the apartment was simply too small. Jacobson then got his family their own apartment upstairs from the Lowners, where he and Alice raised Tom. It gave him time to, as he once put it, "rationalize" the family's situation. They had been uprooted, shocked, and completely disoriented by the move. He and his small family were being supported by Alice's parents because he was not earning any income from his medical practice, but he was embarrassed by having to rely on them for help and support. He had to get back into his medical practice, but how and where? Also, Golder Prague, Slata Praha in Czech, was very different from Berlin and off-putting if one had not grown up there. Jacobson remembered that the Waczlavske Namesti, or Wenzel Street, was almost like a Rodeo Drive in today's Beverly Hills, California—a beautiful thoroughfare with expensive shops that, like parts of the Sunset Strip, rose slowly up a hill to a Hradchin, or castle-like chateau.

Jacobson was entranced by the carnival-like atmosphere of pre-war Prague: the food, the arcades, the desserts, and the coffee houses. It was in the coffee houses that he found social gatherings almost like what the British call "high tea," a late afternoon informal refreshment in which friends and family gathered before continuing with the rest of their day. He was also impressed by the huge ballrooms, which were more than three stories underground. The excavations that carved these out and then decorated them were massive undertakings. Inside the ballrooms, visitors from the rest of Europe, especially Paris, would gather for celebrations.

Because he was not working, Jacobson found he had time to explore the streets of Prague, especially the historical sites in the medieval city. Among other places, he visited the Altneuschul, where the celebrated Kabalistic Rabbi Loew taught and delivered his sermons. In the folklore of eastern Judaism, Rabbi Loew was known as the creator of the Golem, the evil spirit, which would go out into the world and carry out its master's wishes even if it meant inflicting harm on an adversary.

Jacobson's self-enforced prohibition to practice medicine was bothering him. He not only was precluded from treating patients because he had no license in Prague, but also was not engaging in any research at all. Privately, he was treating his wife and her family and a close circle of friends with his concoctions of methamphetamines, vitamins, and animal blood serum, but his practice was not public. However, as word of his energy-boosting injections spread beyond his small circle, new friends began praising his success and created a demand for his medicines, but opening up his practice to the general public would have put him in jeopardy. Because he was safe in Czechoslovakia, he did not seek to break any laws and become persona non grata in the country that had granted him asylum from the Nazis. He decided, therefore, to engage in medical research at the Czechoslovakian University.

Jacobson's opportunity to begin research at the university presented itself in a serendipitous way. He came across an electric heating devise, a cooking utensil, that was essentially an insulated box heated by an electric coil. It gave him the inspiration to create something with which he could sterilize his instruments. He called this new device a Sterotherm, and it became his first patent.

After filing for his patent, Jacobson had to establish proof of concept. Would the device work, first of all, and next, on a practical level, how could the device get him back into medical practice? To establish proof of concept and the medical benefits of the device, he solicited and received the support of Professor Prochazka, director of the Hygienic Institute of the Czech University. He tested the machine with bacterial cultures and spores and found that all of the bacteria and spores were destroyed. The device sterilized the instruments being tested. The test was repeated in the United Kingdom, and the results also confirmed what the Hygienic Institute established. His invention worked to sterilize bacteria-laden instruments. As news spread about the Sterotherm, Jacobson began selling the device to physicians and dentists, all of whom reported that the machine was successful in their respective practices.

His next opportunity to demonstrate the success of the Sterotherm came when he was invited to show off the device in Paris. It also gave him the chance to get out of Prague, where he had become financially dependent on his in-laws, and to return to Paris. He had first visited Paris in 1931, before Hitler's rise to power, where he met Charles Claoué. At that time Jacobson was the official doctor for the German Davis Cup Team.

Claoué was a medical doctor who ran his own plastic surgery clinic and had designed special surgical instruments, which he showed off in a documentary film he had made. He welcomed Jacobson to Paris, demonstrated his interest in Jacobson's sterilization device, and renewed Jacobson's interest in surgery. Jacobson was also impressed by the state of Parisian operating rooms (ORs). In contrast to surgical theaters in Germany, the French ORs were immaculate. Some of the French surgeons, he remembered, reminded him more of butchers than skilled technicians, but their results were excellent. Their methods and the facilities they worked in were far superior to those in Germany. In fact, every aspect of Parisian life was challenging and invigorating to him. Though not a self-proclaimed epicure, Jacobson remembered how impressed he was at the way the French arrayed and presented their food. Food, for the French, was artistic, not just utilitarian.

Jacobson had packed only a little luggage for his stay in Paris and had carried his sterilizer with him, of course. But, even though he said he planned to return to Prague, he only bought a one-way ticket to Paris. For the moment, there was no thought of return to Prague.

By the mid-1930s, Jacobson had settled in France and reestablished his medical practice in Paris, and he continued to develop serums composed of animal blood products, mixtures of vitamins A, B, C, and E, and amphetamines to boost a patient's immunity and provide energy. It was in Paris where he came to a core realization that part of a doctor's role was to make his patients feel good—not just better, but good, a feeling attested to by author Anais Nin. Nin became one of Jacobson's patients in Paris after repeated visits to other doctors had failed to cure her persistent anemia and consequent lack of energy. Nin remarked in her diary, written between 1934 and 1939,[6] that Jacobson's own vigorous and dynamic personality was infectious in itself.

Nin wrote that she had been suffering from what she believed to be bronchitis that her French doctor could not cure. In fact, she would wake up at night coughing until she was almost choking. She was becoming desperate because the lack of sleep and the constant worry over her breathing was interfering with her ability to concentrate, to focus, and to write. Moreover, her constant loss of weight worried her because she did not know how serious her condition was. One of her friends mentioned to her that a refugee doctor from Germany had arrived in Paris and was treating a small group of patients who had made their careers in the arts. Nin made an appointment and visited him in his apartment. She was immediately impressed with him.

Nin said that as soon as she entered Jacobson's apartment, she felt as if she were in the presence of someone unusual. He was animated, alert, and physically vital, she remembered. He was intuitive, unlike doctors she had known who relied on a bedside manner to elicit patient symptoms. His "piercing" and "brilliant" eyes, Nin wrote, immediately struck her, as did his manner. The doctor did not engage in much dialogue and didn't ask for a list of her symptoms. He watched her intently as he examined her, reading her body like a book. Nin described him as a "clairvoyant" who could read a patient's problems as soon as the patient entered the examination room. She was impressed by the fact that Max had none of a doctor's usual mannerisms: the careful listening, the routine pressing of a patient for precise description of symptoms, or the endless testing to make sure there were no mistakes in diagnosis. As if Jacobson could see inside her, he immediately diagnosed Nin as having whooping cough and, she wrote, with only one injection she was brought back to health. Nin wrote that from the moment Jacobson injected her with a substance that made her feel better, she had a "blind faith" not only in his abilities, but also in him as a person. She wanted to become friends and invited Jacobson and Nia Ali to dinner.

Anais Nin believed in free thought. She was not a communist, even though communism was coming into fashion among Europe's intellectual elite. Nin was not especially dogmatic, not aligning her personal philosophy with a political system, but she had friends who were communists. Jacobson, too, soon become friends with many in Nin's circle, acquiring many of them as patients, and soon became associated with communist sympathizers, as well.

Chapter 5

Coming to America

By 1936, Europe was on the verge of war. Hitler was proclaiming "Anschluss" and eyeing the annexation of Austria and the Sudetenland. Jews in Europe who had the means to escape were already leaving, most of them went to the United States. Jacobson was no exception; he emigrated to New York in 1936 because he saw the war clouds drifting over Europe and wanted to be separated from them by an ocean. However, by the time Jacobson had come to the United States, according to his FBI and CIA records, he had become associated with a number of "known Soviet agents." Some of the communist sympathizers identified by the FBI were members of the artistic and literary communities and were more free thinkers, just like Jacobson himself, than political activists—and New York had become a haven for free-thinking artists. The world was still at peace when Dr. Max Jacobson relocated to New York in 1936 and set up practice in Manhattan at East 72nd Street and Third Avenue as a general practitioner. He immediately attracted patients.

Jacobson had written in his diary as early as the 1920s that he was frustrated by the helplessness of his patients who suffered from neuromuscular disease. As he built his new practice in the United States, he continued to study ways of treating the disease. With the drugs he concocted himself, he felt that he could begin to help alleviate his patients' suffering. Jacobson's mantra was that he treated patients, not diseases. He used an individualized combination of hormones, Vitamin B complex, certain enzymes, Vitamins A and E, Vitamin D, Vitamin C, and procaine, a local anesthetic injected intramuscularly (also known under its brand name, Novocaine), depending on each patient's needs. He said that he also recognized through experimentation that small amounts of amphetamines added to his medication increased the medication's therapeutic effect. The amount Jacobson categorized as "small" was twenty milligrams per dose, five times the recommended dosage, but less than the forty milligrams prescribed for alcoholics at that time. It was Jacobson's medical opinion that when methamphetamine was combined with steroids, hormones, and vitamins, it worked differently than when administered by itself.

The addition of methamphetamine to his mixtures, he said, alleviated the heavy fatigue, dizziness, and nausea of medications recommended by medical textbooks at the time. Jacobson claimed that he was able to eliminate such side effects by combining enzymes, steroids, and stimulants along with a drug called Amvitol, which was supposed to remedy physical and mental fatigue and depression. He said that he was encouraged by his initial tests of his drugs on himself to conduct laboratory analyses of his drugs by enlisting the help of the Food and Drug Laboratory in Maspeth, Long Island. From that testing, which helped determine a "bio-essay" of the formula, Jacobson said he found that amphetamines, in combination with vitamins, steroids, and enzymes in proportions configured to each individual patient, eliminated the toxic effects of the amphetamines without diminishing the stimulant effects. Thus, he believed, he was correct in his assumption that he had created an entirely new pharmaceutical compound. At least, that's what he told himself. It allowed him, he believed, to derive the most beneficial effect of amphetamines without any toxicity, with smaller individual doses for each patient, and with doses administered less frequently than the textbook-recommended doses.[24]

He built a laboratory at his office to continue his study of multiple sclerosis and develop his injectable potions, which he would distribute worldwide. Word spread about Dr. Jacobson's special "miraculous treatments" of patients with MS and other neuromuscular diseases, and soon Jacobson was scheduling treatments for patients with MS every Wednesday. His use of an injection with methamphetamine and steroids, which Max called his "vitamin shot," was his drug of choice for his MS patients.

Knowing that there was a growing celebrity community of refugees from Europe, Jacobson was hoping to reach out to them. Soon, many of his former patients from Berlin and Paris, including Anais Nin, Billy Wilder, and Henry Miller, reconnected with him. The treatments, actually stimulants and mood enhancers, that his patients sought were perfectly legal in the 1930s. In fact, in 1937 the American Medical Association approved amphetamine's availability in tablet form, and it was immediately used to treat narcolepsy and the behavioral syndrome called minimal brain dysfunction (MBD). It was also recommended for use by physicians to treat their own fatigue, and in 1940, Burroughs Welcome marketed methamphetamine for the first time under the trade name Methedrine. Later, GlaxoSmithKline entered the lucrative new amphetamine industry with its Dextroamphetamine for use by the military, a drug that later became Adderall and is still in use today as a major drug for the military and the most popular prescription medicine for ADHD in children as well as adults. World War II soldiers in the Allied and Axis forces were given liberal amounts of amphetamines. Pilots, tank drivers, and infantry used Benzedrine, Dexedrine, and Methedrine to stay awake for long periods of time and to enhance levels of courage and bravado.

Starting in the 1940s, usage of amphetamine tablets or Benzedrine by actors and singers to enhance their energy was common, and the drugs were available over the counter. Many German actors had experimented with different type of drugs that were prevalent in Berlin before Hitler. Rumors circulated that actors such as Peter Lorre and Bela Lugosi had experimented with various stimulants to enhance their performances, but ultimately some performers became severely addicted. Many actors used different forms of amphetamine, but Jacobson really took what would become known as "speed" to a whole new level.

When Jacobson began to achieve notoriety among the New York elite starting in the late 1940s, there were no other doctors who had perfected a form of methamphetamine that, in theory, had fewer side effects and was being touted as a miracle drug by celebrity endorsers. There were no drug manufacturers or even any meth labs to service the rich and famous or even the mass public with a "healthy," vitamin-laced, methamphetamine cocktail. Jacobson had the entire market to himself, and he was out to exploit it. He just needed a larger and more influential patient base to spread the word of his wonder drugs.

Author and British historian Dr. Leslie Iversen notes that Jacobson did not substantiate or record his research or observations and subsequently did not publish scholarly papers for scientists to use his work as the basis of treatment. He may have been a pioneer in the creation of methamphetamine, Iversen admits, but Jacobson's lack of a scientific process certainly convoluted his breakthrough in both the creation of the drug and the success in its usage. It is not farfetched to speculate that Jacobson had, by the 1940s, become so influenced by the methamphetamines he was self-injecting that he was more interested in expanding his base of influence with celebrity patients than he was in documenting his research in a scientific or scholarly way.

Soon after relocating to New York, tensions at home with Alice had mounted and risen to a boiling point, leading to their eventual divorce. His personal life improved, however, when he reconnected with Nina Hagen, who had also emigrated to the United States. Max had fallen in love with Nina when they first met in Germany after she had taken a bad fall from a horse. She was still a young teenager then, but Max had become enchanted with her. By 1945, in the afterglow of the defeat of Nazi Germany and a new start in America, he fell in love with Nina all over again, and they married in 1946 and had a daughter, Jill, who was born on September 22, 1947.

In 1946, Jacobson established a corporation named the Constructive Research Foundation for the ostensible purpose of researching and ultimately curing neuromuscular diseases such as MS when, in fact, he was using the foundation as a façade to purchase vast amounts of the raw materials to make and distribute his injectable concoctions. It was a profitable venture, even though the corporation was established as a nonprofit, and kept Jacobson solvent while he claimed that he was undertaking purely altruistic research. His lucrative business came at a personal and professional cost, however.

Although Jacobson had initially had hospital privileges in New York, he was denied access to those hospitals starting in 1946 due to what the hospitals' medical administrators determined were his "irregular" treatments. Accordingly, although he had remained a member of the American Medical Association until 1971, he had to refer his patients to other doctors if they needed surgery or hospital care. "Max always experimented with his mixtures on himself, before he applied it to any patient," recalled Mike Samek,[7] talking about his friend's willingness to experience what he thought his patients would experience. However, it was eagerness for self-experimentation that would eventually be one of the charges leveled at him during his New York state medical license revocation hearings thirty years later.

By the late 1940s, Jacobson's office became a Venus flytrap for countless numbers of celebrities from all spheres. There was future vice president Nelson Rockefeller and senator Claude Pepper; opera stars Leontyne Price, Maria Callas, and Paul Robeson; sportscaster Mel Allen; physicist Dr. Niels Bohr; composer Leonard Bernstein; actors Eddie Fisher and Ingrid Bergman; jazz singer Mabel Mercer; playwright George S. Kaufman; and choreographer and director Bob Fosse, just to name a few. One of Jacobson's most powerful and high-profile patients was the Hollywood director Cecil B. DeMille.

Jacobson himself said that he had stabilized his practice by the early 1950s with a functioning office staffed with a receptionist and assistants. It was around this time he was faced with an emergency concerning a major Hollywood motion picture, *The Ten Commandments,* and the impact it was having on director DeMille, who was in trouble with Paramount, the studio making the film. DeMille was over budget, and during the filming he had suffered a serious heart attack. Attending to him was a local physician, Dr. Hussein Ibrahim, as well as Max Jacobson, whom DeMille had flown to the set on location in Egypt. Both doctors advised DeMille that his recovery would require four weeks of bed rest, but his response was, "Forget it, gentlemen. I'm going to the set in the morning." So he and Jacobson worked out a plan that would enable him to continue directing with as little physical stress as possible. And as long as the director's spirits were high from methamphetamine, it worked. When dysentery began afflicting workers on the set, DeMille said, according to Scott Eyman in *The Empire of Dreams: The Epic Life of Cecil B. DeMille*,[8] "Most of us have suffered from dysentery, which we did not seem able to cure, so I sent for Dr. Max Jacobson to come in from New York. He flew out here with Yul Brynner . . . he has been here for four days now and we are all in much better shape. . . . As you know, he is one of the best doctors in America, and I felt the situation was sufficiently important to bring him on my personal expense, which I did." In fact, DeMille was so enamored with the results of Jacobson's injections and their ability to increase energy levels that when it came time for him to shoot the scene in which actor Charlton Heston, portraying Moses, receives the Ten Commandments on Mount Sinai, DeMille asked Jacobson to give Heston an injection, to which request Jacobson obliged.

Writer and director Billy Wilder said he'd met Jacobson again on a flight with Cecil B. DeMille to Egypt when DeMille was on location. Jacobson, he said "pumps him full of amphetamine magic shots so that DeMille can still climb ladders and shoot the scenes with maybe six thousand extras standing around."[9]

After principal photography on *The Ten Commandments* was

completed, DeMille returned to the United States for editing and post production. However, DeMille had become saddened by the death of his brother in March 1955 and summoned Jacobson to Hollywood, where the doctor demanded that DeMille decrease his schedule and relegate the film editing to someone else. Jacobson's treatment seemed to restore DeMille's professional abilities, and his optimism was further restored after he had seen the first cut of *The Ten Commandments.* As the schedule for the release and promotion of the film was finalized, and the studio told DeMille he had to promote the film personally in foreign markets as well as in the United States, DeMille demanded that Jacobson travel with him to keep up his energy. Together, they would meet with Pope Pius XII in Rome, German Chancellor Conrad Adenauer, the mayor of Berlin Willy Brandt, and Queen Elizabeth and Winston Churchill in England. It was a junket that took Jacobson back to the Europe of his youth.

Jacobson, who was always happy to be in the midst of pomp and ceremony, was especially impressed at DeMille's treatment in Rome. They were met by the chief representative of Paramount Studios in Italy, who led the group to their suite in the Hotel Excelsior, one of the premier hotels in Rome. Jacobson was especially impressed at how much the hotel suite had been set up for DeMille's predilections, including a rocking chair and other amenities. One morning, Jacobson found DeMille on the balcony of the hotel room rehearsing for his meeting with Pope Pius XII. He was so engrossed in the moment as he practiced his presentation that he hadn't noticed the crowd gathering in the street below. When Jacobson pointed this out, DeMille waved embarrassedly and went back inside to his rocking chair. DeMille's practice paid off the next day, when DeMille's audience with the Pope at the summer residence at

Castel Gondolfo was confirmed, and DeMille invited his secretary, his daughter, and her husband, the Paramount representatives in Italy, and Jacobson and his wife, Nina, to come along. On their arrival at the papal residence, the group was led into a large reception hall with huge red tapestries hanging from the walls and brightly decorated carpets on the floor. There they awaited the pope, who entered from an ante room.

A cardinal introduced the group to the Holy Father, and each person bowed when his or name was announced. The instructions to the group had been for them to wait until the Pope spoke before they addressed him. It was the protocol; however, DeMille started speaking immediately about how important his movie was and why it was especially important to the Italian people. Pope Pius nodded politely, perhaps surprised at the outspokenness of this American motion picture director, until the exasperated cardinal sputtered, "Ecco, ecco," (enough, enough), and ushered the group toward the exit. As they left, DeMille realized he had almost forgotten the reason for the visit and turned back to present the Pope with an $8,000 check for charity. His mission was done.

The group's next stop was Berlin. Less than a decade after the Berlin Airlift, during which Nina's brother had been killed, and more than a decade after Jacobson's escape from Nazi Germany, Jacobson found himself in a city where he had almost been killed had he not fled after the warning from the brown-shirted storm trooper.

After they landed in Germany, the DeMille group drove to Hotel, Am Zoo in the Western sector of Berlin, where they met Jacobson's former nurse. His old office had been right near the hotel, but was now gone. In its place Jacobson saw a bomb crater that he noted in his diaries as very deep, almost the size of a building.

That evening, there was a dinner reception with several government officials in attendance in the meeting hall of the new Jewish community, at which DeMille was expected to give a speech. He was reluctant, even though Jacobson had brought DeMille's petit mal seizures under control with his drugs. But DeMille's worries proved to be prophetic, and the tense atmosphere of the reception was almost too much for him. Jacobson guessed that the audience attributed the forty-five seconds of silence as DeMille stood there, actually unconscious on his feet, to the emotional content of his address. But DeMille regained his senses after the seizure and continued his presentation. The trip to Berlin was tense, and Jacobson was relieved when their stay in the city came to an end.

The Jacobsons' next stop was in Bonn, where Nina Hagen's family had been very helpful to German Chancellor Adenauer twenty years earlier before the war and had essentially launched his career in banking. When Nina and Jacobson arrived at Adenauer's office in Bonn as part of the DeMille entourage, they went directly to the Chancellor's office at the Auswärtige Amt, the German equivalent of the U.S. State Department. When the Chancellor saw Nina, he embraced her, and ushered the Jacobsons into his office for a private conversation. Jacobson was interested in Adenauer's relationship with his former mentor Dr. Niehans, asking the chancellor if he had been treated by him. Niehans was one of the inventors of cellular therapy. When Max was a medical student and then an intern, he studied Niehans's theories about the rejuvenative process that takes place in living cells and sought to adapt them to his practice of internal medicine. It was Dr. Niehans who inspired Max's early research in cellular therapy.

Jacobson remembered that Asenauer told him that he had seen

him several times," without any further elaboration, and then closed down the conversation. They left his private office to find DeMille's entourage fidgeting restlessly in the reception area. They had a flight to catch. Their next stop was Shannon Airport in Ireland en route to London.

Before the DeMille group had left the United States for the trip to Europe, one of Sir Winston Churchill's aides, who was concerned over the condition of Sir Winston, believed that the prime minister could benefit from a consultation with Jacobson and had arranged in advance a meeting between him and Lord Moran, Churchill's personal physician. When the DeMille entourage arrived at the Dorchester Hotel in London, the desk informed Jacobson that Lord Moran was in the lobby. Jacobson invited him up to DeMille's suite, where the director had already changed into a bathrobe. Lord Moran knew all about DeMille's heart attacks and asked him why he refused to follow the standard guidelines for recovery. At that, DeMille threw off his bathrobe and proceeded to do a dozen pushups. When he got up, he said, "Does this answer your question?" As he strutted out of the room, he muttered, "I am a good example of Dr. Jacobson's way of treating people." Lord Moran asked Jacobson what he had prescribed for DeMille, and, without hesitation, Jacobson gave him a detailed summary of the medication and how he prescribed it while Moran scribbled notes on a pad. Jacobson said he didn't believe in a soft bedside manner but rather a direct approach that demanded his patients to follow his specific, albeit unorthodox, instructions. Their conversation turned next to Churchill, who was uncooperative when it came to medical treatment. Jacobson made some suggestions, recommended some of the formulas he used, and said that he had been successful treating patients who were difficult. Lord Moran thanked Jacobson for the suggestions. Later that day, the DeMille entourage had an audience with a young Queen Elizabeth, attended a royal command performance, and headed back to the airport for the flight to New York and then to Los Angeles in time for the theatrical release of *The Ten Commandments.*

Despite all of DeMille's worrying, *The Ten Commandments* was an unqualified success and earned Academy Award nominations for best picture and best actor, Charlton Heston. That film would be the last one DeMille would ever direct. After suffering from another heart attack, he turned over the directing reins on his next picture, *The Buccaneer,* to his son-in-law, Anthony Quinn. When Jacobson saw DeMille again, it was at the Waldorf Astoria in Manhattan, where DeMille had a meeting with one of the heads of Paramount to terminate his contract with the studio. It would also be the last time Jacobson would ever see DeMille alive.

DeMille had been seeing Jacobson occasionally since 1952, but no one in DeMille's inner circle seemed to know or care what Jacobson was prescribing; they knew only that it banished DeMille's fatigue and made sleep optional. Jacobson's manner and thriving medical practice gave him an aura of omnipotence that wasn't to be found in the usual dispenser of pep pills that were epidemic in Hollywood in the 1940s. Tennessee Williams would write that the doctor had "a magical atmosphere of understanding and compassion. . . . I don't think he ever took my blood pressure or my pulse or had me fill out a form about my medical history. He just looked at me . . . then started concocting a shot, drawing a bit of fluid from one bottle and another as my suspense and my alarm increased. But the aftermath of the injection was almost miraculous.

I felt as if a concrete sarcophagus about me had sprung open and I was released as a bird on a wing."[10] Williams's response was not unusual; one female patient described the effects of the injection as resembling an orgasm.

Cecil's adopted son, Richard DeMille, however, smelled a rat. "Max Jacobson was what we would now call a guru. He was slightly mysterious and always had the latest medical information and spoke in a technical language that had a great sound to it. He was a total charlatan."[11] Henry Noerdlinger, who was more sophisticated than most of the people on DeMille's staff, was on to Jacobson fairly quickly. Noerdlinger remembers going into a tent in Egypt with Jacobson one day, and, without a word, the doctor said, "Don't tell me. I know what's wrong with you," whereupon he produced a syringe, had Noerdlinger drop his pants, and gave him a shot.

"He was a most peculiar doctor," (as quoted by Eyman in *Empire of Dreams*) Noerdlinger would say to anyone who asked him. When Joan Brooskin, a member of the crew on *The Ten Commandments*, came down with dengue fever, Jacobson gave her a couple of shots and told her that not only would she get over the fever, but "she would never have migraines or menstrual cramps again!"[12]

"When DeMille's energy lagged, he would pick himself up with a shot of Dr. Feelgood's juice," remembered DeMille's son-in-law, actor Anthony Quinn. "He was hooked and so was Katherine," Quinn said about his wife.[13] "She even started taking the children to Dr. Feelgood." Quinn, too, began seeing Jacobson for pick-me-ups. DeMille's increasing dependency on his drug-pushing doctor, attested to by the unquestioned respect in his correspondence to Jacobson, would be the most obvious manifestation of a naivete that Donald Hayne, a crew member on a number of motion pictures, had observed: "The latest glib expert to come along can make an impression on DeMille, at least if he proclaims an expertise in a field that DeMille is unfamiliar."[2514]

There are many stories about Jacobson's influence among celebrities on both the West and East Coasts. If his unacknowledged strategy was to exert greater control over an ever-widening circle of patients, it was working.

Chapter 6

Milton Blackstone, Eddie Fisher, and the Tragic Undoing of Bob Cummings

The hype surrounding the powerful feel-good elixir formulated by Max Jacobson was spreading through the artistic community of New York in the early 1950s. But when Jacobson met show business promoter Milton Blackstone, the doctor's influence via Blackstone's network spread like a virus through the entertainment industry. The story of their relationship began at a small resort in the Catskill Mountains, just two hours north of Manhattan.

Jacobson was still a young man studying medicine in Berlin in the 1920s when Jennie Grossinger and her husband Harry, who was also her first cousin, purchased more than one hundred acres of farmland and built a small hotel in the Catskill Mountains, soon to become known as the Borscht Belt, and a starting point for many great comedians of the 1950s. Milton Blackstone, a young hustling advertising promoter in the 1930s, whose real name was Moshe Schwartzstein, had been a frequent guest at the hotel and became fast friends with Jennie, whom he convinced to expand the hotel beyond its Jewish clientele. It was thought by many that Blackstone and Jennie were lovers. However, the truth was that Blackstone was gay and Jennie was his cover, according to screen writer and producer Rocky Kalish.[15]

During the years of the Great Depression, Blackstone, who was a master at promotion, began using different types of gimmicks to attract guests to make the long drive from enclaves in the Bronx and Brooklyn up the country roads along the southern tier of New York State to the Catskill resort. Blackstone also used his connections in the sports world to bring sports writers up to the new resort and even convinced lightweight boxing champ Barney Ross to open his training camp there.

In 1934, Blackstone's star was on the rise, and he was able to attract many Broadway celebrities to Grossinger's. Soon the show business columnists arrived, and the hotel became a celebrity stop where Broadway and nightclub personalities could hobnob informally with the columnists and reviewers who could promote their reputations. And at the center of it all was Milton Blackstone.

With cash in the form of loans, raised by Milton Blackstone from his financial sources, Grossinger's quickly became a world-class resort by the 1940s and began paying back the loan from Milton Blackstone. The money was delivered to Blackstone's employee, Austin "Rocky" Kalish, a young man who would soon become the television screenwriter for episodes of *F Troop, Family Affair, Maude,* and *Good Times.*

When Blackstone became Jacobson's patient in the mid-1940s, he spread the word about the doctor's special vitamin shot that increased a person's energy level. Blackstone said it was almost like magic. Singer Eddie Fisher once said, "Max and Milton were exact opposites. Loud and arrogant, Max didn't care how he looked or what he said."[16] All that mattered was that Jacobson could cure whatever ailed a patient with a single injection, which made the patient feel good. The word spread, and Jacobson started to add patients from the entertainment industry to his list. Within a very short time he became the "in" doctor for singers who lost their voice, actors who needed to get over the jitters, authors who suffered from writer's block, and politicians before important speeches. All types of public performers were becoming patients, and soon business in Max's office was standing room only.

The relationship between Milton Blackstone and Max Jacobson soon flourished, with Rocky Kalish acting as the go-between, picking up bags of preloaded medicine syringes from Max's office and bringing them over to Blackstone's New York office or up to Grossinger's, where he also had an office. And, according to Kalish,[17] Blackstone Advertising began to flourish as well. Blackstone had turned Grossinger's into a world-class resort, reaching out beyond its Jewish clientele who came for the kosher gehaimishe food to the entertainers who would transform television in the 1950s and 1960s and to sports greats such as the boxing champions who trained there, including Rocky Marciano, Ingemar Johannson, Max Baer, and welterweight Barney Ross.

Another one of Blackstone's clients was vaudeville, motion picture, and night club comedian and singer Eddie Cantor, whose trademark song was "If You Knew Susie." Cantor had his own television show in the 1950s and was always looking for new talent. One of the performers Blackstone identified for Cantor was singer and local heartthrob Eddie Fisher. In a typical Blackstone stunt, he made an arrangement with Jennie Grossinger to bring Cantor to the resort to meet Eddie Fisher, a lifeguard at Grossingers as well as an aspiring entertainer. The deal was simple: If Eddie's performance before the Grossinger audience was successful—that is, if the audience liked him—Cantor would agree to give Fisher a national television debut on his show. But to make sure that Fisher's performance was popular, the Grossinger nieces and their friends circulated among the audience with instructions to get the crowd to cheer wildly when Fisher completed his number. It was a set-up, but it worked, and when Eddie Cantor, who knew all about the arrangement, saw the audience reaction, he got up and announced that he would invite Eddie Fisher to sing on his show. Eddie was a hit; he began making records and more television appearances, and thus was a legend created. Eddie Fisher became Milton Blackstone's protégé.

Blackstone encouraged Eddie Fisher to find ways to pump up his energy because he wanted to tour Fisher around the country to promote his record albums. To facilitate that, Blackstone cemented the relationship between Fisher and Jacobson and, in Eddie Fisher's own words,[18] Jacobson became a "second father" to him, providing him with as many special injections as he needed to keep him going.

As Milton Blackstone's influence grew in the entertainment industry, so did Max Jacobson's connection to artists and performers. Max was already treating writers Truman Capote, Tennessee Williams, Rod Serling, and one of modern America's most important screenwriters and playwrights, Paddy Chayefsky, whose screenplay *Network* predicted the rise of corporate ownership of the media, the merging of news and entertainment, and even reality television shows themselves.

Rod Serling was also one of the most prolific television writers of the 1950s, creating teleplays for *Playhouse 90, Kraft,* and other dramatic, long-form television series before his series *The Twilight Zone,* which led him to become friends with Chayefsky. Serling and Chayefsky had the same agent, Blanche Gaines, who was one of

Max's patients, as well, and brought Chayefsky to Max first. Then, either Gaines or Chayefsky introduced Rod Serling to Jacobson. Rod quickly became a Jacobson repeat patient, which, though ultimately destructive, enabled him to write at a furious pace as well as produce *The Twilight Zone*. Rod Serling's family, whom we sought to interview for this book, dispute that Rod Serling was addicted to methamphetamine.

One of Max Jacobson's most unfortunate victims was Serling's friend, actor Bob Cummings, who starred in a 1960 episode of *The Twilight Zone*. Cummings most likely became connected to Max Jacobson before he met Rod Serling, though, because by the time he appeared on *The Twilight Zone*, he was already a meth addict. According to Del Reisman, Rod Serling's script supervisor on *Twilight Zone*, Reisman was present at dinner between Serling and Robert Cummings, who was performing in an episode titled "King Nine Will Not Return." At the dinner, Reisman recalled in an interview, Cummings remarked to Serling about the thick steak smothered in onions he was eating and the cigarettes he was smoking that Serling wouldn't live to be fifty at the rate he was going. Serling said to Cummings, according to Reisman, "you and I go to the same doctor and we both take the same shit he's giving us. So don't criticize me." It was an admission in Serling's own words that he was a Jacobson patient receiving the same drugs as was Cummings. And the drugs contained high doses of methamphetamine. Cummings's connection to Jacobson was most likely through his friendship with singer Rosemary Clooney and her husband, actor Jose Ferrer, who were both Jacobson patients. Rosemary Clooney's nephew, George Clooney, who said that his aunt had gone into decline towards the end of her career, could not determine whether that decline was a result of her relationship with Max Jacobson and his methamphetamine injections.[19] But regardless of who introduced Cummings to Jacobson, it was a relationship that destroyed Cummings's career as well as his life.

The story of Bob Cummings is one of the great Hollywood tragedies that mark the path of devastation traveled by many of Max Jacobson's patients, including screen legend Marilyn Monroe. The story of Cummings's descent is a classic example of how destructive methamphetamines can be, not just because of drug dependency but also because the downside of a methamphetamine high is a near-clinical depression. It was that depression that caused Cummings's downward spiral until he was unable to care for himself.

Robert Cummings was one of the great film and television actors of the mid-twentieth century. From Academy Award–winning films such as *Kings Row*, in which he played out one of the most homoerotic scenes in motion pictures with future president Ronald Reagan, to Hitchcock's *Saboteur* and *Dial M For Murder*, to television's *Love That Bob*, Cummings was Hollywood royalty during the 1940s and 1950s. He maintained his youthful appearance through his regimen of exercise and health foods, and his book, *Stay Young and Vital*,[20] became a national bestseller. Yet his secret addiction to Jacobson's elixir was kept closeted for more than fifty years.

How did Cummings get hooked on methamphetamines? Bob started with Max Jacobson in 1954 when he was in New York to do the CBS anthology series *Studio One* in the first and original production of Reginald Rose's *Twelve Angry Men,* which later became a feature film starring Henry Fonda and Lee J. Cobb. Rose was also a client of Blanche Gaines, the agent for Rod Serling and Paddy Chayefsky. Rose, as did Rosemary Clooney and her jusband José Ferrar, recommended Jacobson to Cummings, who quickly became addicted to the drug. On his visit to New York City, he scheduled a visit to Jacobson's office, where he complained to Jacobson about a loss of energy. Jacobson suggested to Cummings his therapy of "a B-12 mixture of vitamin shots." He assured Cummings, who liked to know the contents of anything he took, that the formula would be a mixture of vitamins and other ingredients such as "sheep sperm" and "monkey gonads." Jacobson claimed that the formula he used in his injections made him the modern incarnation of Ponce de León, delivering the fountain of youth to his patients. He firmly believed that his concoction would help Cummings's stamina and arouse his sexual desire, as well.

A couple of assumptions can be made regarding Cummings's knowledge of what "Magic Max's" serum consisted of. First, Cummings was the son of a physician and was not totally naive about medicine, legitimate or otherwise. He was very well-read on the subject of vitamins and supplements, had experimented with many of them, and was very aware of their effects. Second, by the time he became Jacobson's patient, he most likely had heard the scuttlebutt from other patients who believed the injections contained methamphetamines, but Cummings was so pleased with the results that he most likely ignored what he might have suspected the true contents were. By the time he was addicted to the mixture, it was too late.

Dwayne Hickman, Cummings's co-star on *The Bob Cummings Show,* who later starred in his own television series, *The Many Loves of Dobie Gillis,* based on Max Shulman's collection of short stories by the same name, was the first to reveal Bob's dark side. Hickman remembered a publicity jaunt for the series when he accompanied Cummings to New York, where Bob took Hickman for a visit to his favorite physician:

Bob told me this doctor gave him health injections that were loaded with vitamins, sheep sperm, and monkey gonads. He told me that this was this doctor's discovery of the fountain of youth. What was unusual about his office was that the patients that were in the office included Anthony Quinn, Tennessee Williams, and others that Bob pointed out to me. The doctor came out to greet Bob, and his lab coat was rather filthy and spotted with blood. It was a long day, and Bob kind of dragged along with the doctor. When he came out of the office about thirty minutes later, there was a definite bounce to his step. He had tremendous energy. He offered me an injection and said, "Chuck, I'll pay for a treatment for you," to which I politely declined.[21]

Dwayne's revelation about Cummings's addiction to methamphetamines opened the floodgates, and friends, family, and fellow actors finally came clean about the sordid last years of Cummings's life, which were the direct result of Jacobson's treatment.

Celebrated television host Art Linkletter, who defined audience-participation television in the 1950s and who hosted *House Party* and *Kids Say the Darndest Things,* was instrumental in helping save his longtime friend's life:

Bob and I had been the closest of friends for many years. . . . Starting in the late 1950s and early 1960s I noticed a strong change in Bob's personality. . . . He was like a megalomaniac and quite belligerent. He really had these delusions of grandeur. He was rather a happy-go-lucky type of guy, but he would argue till he was blue in the face about his strong belief in health foods that he learned from his father. When I told Mary [Bob's wife] about this, she broke down about the drugs he was taking. I stayed out of the fray, but noticed that

Bob was getting progressively worse. I never discussed the drugs or who was supplying him. I know I should have, as I later learned with my daughter's suicide [Linkletter's daughter, Diane, committed suicide after consuming drugs and jumping from her apartment window in 1969]. Later, around 1965, Mary asked [for] my help with Bob. There were no drug confrontations [interventions] as there are today, so I arranged for Bob to be committed to a psychiatric hospital. I came over to their house, and Bob was dressing for an awards dinner. I remember this clearly, as Bob fought hard as they put him in a straight-jacket and took him off screaming. Our relationship was severely strained after that. I think he blamed Mary for this as well, and he never forgave her. He was in the clinic for a couple months, as I remember. I don't think he ever got off the drugs. It truly destroyed his life.[22]

As Bob's addiction from Jacobson's drugs spiraled out of control, his life began to unravel. Because Bob lived on the West Coast and Jacobson was in New York, Jacobson had his son, Dr. Thomas Jacobson, deliver the magic potion. By this time, Bob was self-injecting the drug in his ankle and had gone far beyond Max's prescribed dose. Julie Newmar, who played the Catwoman on the series *Batman* and who was Bob's costar in the short-lived 1960s television series *My Living Doll,* said that Bob had frantically pushed her to self-inject the magic elixir as well, but she refused. On that series, Bob constantly fought with producers because he was competing for camera time with the young and vivacious Newmar, even as he was hobbled by his reliance on meth injections. He became erratic and soon was confronting everyone on the set.

According to television producer Bob Finkel, the executive producer of the new Cummings show:

> Bob was very erratic to deal with. I was hired by Lew Wasserman and MCA/Universal to produce the series. Bob tried to direct every episode and was incredibly moody. I had heard only good things about him, so I was rather surprised. It was a very difficult series to mount. I remember this poor little guy named Eddie Rubin, who worked for Bob as his assistant. Bob would send him over with new directives, and he would be quite submissive with his approach. I was not aware of Bob's drug problem, and it would have explained many of the problems we had with him.[23]

Cummings's life continued to unravel. His wife Mary had invested much of their fortune in supposedly "tax-free" Swiss bank accounts. The IRS began a long investigation into their investments, which turned out to be illegal avoidance schemes. All of this played heavily on Cummings's psyche, pushing him further into a depression that was only made worse by the methamphetamines.

Cummings not only continued but accelerated his injections of Max's elixir. However, his TV likability quotient was still very high. When television producer Jack Chertok was asked to create a high-concept series like *Bewitched,* he created *My Living Doll,* which was about a gorgeous female robot who lived with an Army psychiatrist. CBS hired actress Julie Newmar for the female lead, and Chertok wanted either Efrem Zimbalist Jr. of *77 Sunset Strip* or Bob Crane of *Hogan's Heroes* to play the male lead. The head of CBS insisted on Cummings, and even though the concept for the show was good, Cummings proved to be unreliable.

Cummings's use of methamphetamine was out of control by

the time the series started filming in August 1964. Not only was Cummings getting too old for the male romantic leads he was playing, but he was also depressed, and Jacobson's drugs were seriously impairing his behavior, professionally as well as personally.

"I had directed Bob earlier in his career, but by the time I directed him in *Beach Party* (1963)," he had changed," said William Asher, the celebrated director of *I Love Lucy* and *Bewitched*. "I did not hear of the drug use until much later, but at that time I was not aware."[24]

By the time Bob was starring in *My Living Doll*, he was completely out of control on the set. He fought with directors, writers, and the producer, Jack Chertok. It was as if there was something else directing his behavior, said his costar, Julie Newmar.

Newmar says she still has painful memories of Cummings on the series:

I clearly knew that he was using drugs. He called them "vitamin shots." However, I saw him clearly injecting the syringes. He had a mad burst of energy soon thereafter. He ruined many scenes that were quite difficult. He offered me the injections. I worked hard to conquer the role of Rhonda, but he ruined many scenes. He was outdated. His type of shtick was old hat. Everyone was aware of his drug use and his erratic behavior. There was no doubt his intent was to try to take the focus off my character and make him[self] the central core of the show. It was a very difficult situation. Bob was unhappy that I was drawing more attention. I think he felt he was being pushed into a secondary role and his career was slipping away. It became so difficult, I rented an apartment across from the studio as I spent all of my hours devoted to the show. I was a method-trained actress from the Actor's Studio. I studied with Strasberg, and my style clashed with him. He had that '50's type of shtick. He wanted to be the writer, director, and producer. He clashed with everyone on the production."[25]

Cummings demanded a meeting with Chertok about his spec script and his role on the series. He was going to force his hand, as he felt he was the star of the program. However, CBS boss Jim Aubrey was keeping an eye on the ratings, which were fading fast. Aubrey also admired the talent of young Julie Newmar and believed that Cummings was excess baggage and had to be eliminated to salvage the show. When Cummings walked into the meeting, he was surprised to find not only Chertok but also Aubrey waiting for him.

Cummings, his career in steep decline, an anachronism in television comedy, and completely compromised by his addiction to Max Jacobson's injections, was now going to face the same treatment that others in show business had before him. Cummings gave his ultimatum: either they produce his spec script and change the focus of the show or he was walking. Cummings had set himself up, and Aubrey pounced. He told Cummings that he was aware of his drug use and his relationship with Dr. Feelgood, and that not only was he firing Cummings from the series, but he was also going to spread the news throughout the industry that Cummings was a drug addict. And, true to his word, Aubrey did just that. Cummings became persona non grata in the industry, uninsurable and undependable, and, ultimately, unhirable. It was a precipitous fall from grace.

Disconsolate and living from injection to injection, Cummings took a job in a cheap Hong Kong karate film called *Five Golden Dragons*. On the set, he met a young script girl named Gina (or GeeGee) Fong. Cummings and Fong became inseparable. When Cummings called his wife to ask whether he could bring Fong home to work as his secretary,

Mary was amenable, but it was a decision she would later regret. After Mary learned that Cummings was having an affair with Fong and Font was pregnant with his child, Cummings moved out of their Beverly Hills home to live with Fong and her daughter in a cramped apartment.

After nearly forty years in films, television, and radio, Cummings had no career. In desperate need of money, he purchased an RV and took Fong and her daughter, whom he had adopted, on the road, picking up gigs wherever he could by following the nomadic life of an actor playing small parts in dinner theaters across the United States. He kept working because he needed money, not only for his new family but also for his ongoing drug addiction through his supplier Dr. Jacobson.

Bob's seven children were also acutely aware of Bob's addiction. They all watched as their father went from being an A-list star with a substantial income who lived in a beautiful home in Beverly Hills to near-poverty at the end of his life, when he lived at the shabby Horace Heidt Apartments in Sherman Oaks subsisting on only his pension.

After Bob moved out of the family home in Beverly Hills, Mary hired noted divorce attorney Marvin Mitchelson in what became one of the most bitter public divorces of the 1960s. Their divorce, granted on January 15, 1970, was one of the first finalized under California's "no fault" divorce law, where they divided what was left in community property assets of approximately $700,000. As the parties fought over the assets of the marriage, the IRS seized the Cummings' Beverly Hills home, took title, and evicted Mary and the children who still remained at home. The IRS also seized much of Cummings's substantial fortune for back taxes owed on funds invested in offshore accounts that were not recorded and for huge penalties assessed on the money that was owed in taxes but never paid.

Cummings fled from Los Angeles, and by the early 1970s he and his new family had moved to the Marin County area of San Francisco. When Jacobson stopped distributing around 1975, Bob went to the Bahamas to hook up a new connection for meth.

By the mid-1980s, Bob had been forgotten in Hollywood. His health had spiraled downward with the combination of his continued drug use and a diagnosis of Parkinson's disease. Fong, who was about thirty-five years younger than Bob, was not about to be slowed down by this now aged partner, and she divorced Cummings in 1987.

Alone and very depressed, Cummings moved into the Horace Heidt Magnolia Estates apartment complex that was built by radio bandleader Horace Heidt for retired and "down on their luck" musicians in Sherman Oaks. A longtime resident said about the complex, "This place is so kitsch that it's hard to believe it's withstood the test of time. Imagine a miniature golf course, a retirement community, and 'It's a Small World' all rolled into one."

Bob had a difficult time living without assistance after his onset of Parkinson's disease and his continued drug use. Longtime friend Milton Berle observed this. He went through the fan mail that Bob received and told him he would select a new wife from his list of fans—someone who could take care of Bob.

"I picked some girl from . . . Tennessee that was a cashier at a Piggly Wiggly store. Bob loved big tits, so I picked this cashier who sent her picture. We took her information to his astrologer, who approved of the match. We paid for this . . . hillbilly to fly out here and marry Bob and become his caretaker. She was a real . . . mieskeit." [26]

Thus Martha "Janie" Burzynski became the fifth and final Mrs. Robert Cummings, having flown out to Los Angeles and married the aging Cummings. She had had stars in her eyes and believed her dream of living the Hollywood life had come true. However, she had not married the suave Bob Cummings of television and movies. Instead, she wound up with "Grandpa Collins," a semi-invalid drug addict who had been forced into a twilight retirement by his addiction. It was not a match made in heaven. Instead, the angry Janie Cummings tormented her aged husband who, when he realized the intensity of her distress at the marriage and began to suffer the physical abuse she inflicted on him, lived in constant terror of this cashier from the Piggly Wiggly.

Cummings, now tired of the abuse he was receiving from the belligerent Janie, filed for divorce. Bob then entered the Motion Picture Home in Woodland Hills, California, where he died on December 2, 1990. Although his death certificate claimed his death occurred from renal failure, his body was battered from the effect of Parkinson's and more than thirty years of the effects of methamphetamines.

It was a tragic ending for one of Hollywood's greatest stars, whose television career had earned him worldwide fame and millions of dollars per year with both his ownership and fees of *Love That Bob*. Many of Cummings's friends and family say this sad tale was just one of many that was triggered by the magic elixir of Dr. Max Jacobson.

The ever-blunt Milton Berle said of Jacobson, "That [jerk] killed him. I met that [piece of trash] with Fisher in Vegas. That [jerk] should have been hung up by his . . . balls for what he did." (Obscenities replaced by editor.)[27] By then, however, Max Jacobson had become responsible, both directly and indirectly, for many more deaths. The hypergrandiosity brought on by the drugs he was self-injecting would drive Jacobson's needle into the throat of senator and Democratic presidential candidate John F. Kennedy.

Chapter 7

The Vienna Summit

Just a few short months after his inauguration, the young President Kennedy, now firmly addicted to Jacobson's medication, faced two tough tests: the Bay of Pigs invasion, which had been initiated under President Eisenhower, and the Vienna Summit with Nikita Khrushchev. The president knew that the Soviet premier would be looking to exploit any weakness and any vulnerability that he could. Kennedy had to be strong, vigorous, and resistant to any threats. JFK needed all the help he could get.

Given the president's medical history and the efficacy of Max Jacobson's treatments, not to take the doctor with him on the trip to meet with Soviet premier Khrushchev was unthinkable. However, Jacobson and his wife would not be traveling on Air Force One with the president, but rather on an Air France flight. There was too much risk of press scrutiny, the White House said, with the prying eyes of reporters wanting to know who was traveling with the presidential party on Air Force One on this all-important but very tough trip. Even though Kennedy felt prepared and had had many discussions with his secretary of state Dean Rusk about how Khrushchev might behave, the president was nevertheless nervous. And why shouldn't he be? The Vienna Summit, which Kennedy had first proposed in February 1961, would be held in the shadow of the failed invasion of Cuba.

The Bay of Pigs invasion of April 17, 1961, was an unmitigated disaster, a miscalculation by the CIA that put the new president, who had green-lighted the operation, at a severe disadvantage when facing Khrushchev across a conference table. The plan was doomed from the start because, although the preparations for the invasion were supposedly put into motion in complete secrecy, the operation was quickly the topic of conversation among the Cuban exile community around Miami. It didn't take long for Castro's intelligence service to learn of the plan.

Khrushchev was publicly outraged, but secretly believed that the young president who had stumbled so badly could easily be pushed around. Thus, Kennedy, needing to be strong, had asked Jacobson to come along, hoping that what the doctor did for him in the debates would sustain him in his face-to-face meeting with an angry and brutal Soviet premier.

If Jacobson initially thought that this trip and the days leading up to it would go smoothly, he would be proven wrong. Not too long before he left the country, he and his friend Mike Samek came back to Jacobson's office late one night to find that the place had been ransacked. Samek later described the scene of devastation: Vials of liquid had been overturned, furniture moved around, and confidential patient files strewn everywhere. It didn't take Samek long to figure out what had happened. It was the KGB (the Russian Committee for State Security), he told Jacobson. The KGB, knowing that Kennedy was Max's patient, was looking for information on the president's physical and mental condition. They knew who Jacobson was, Samek said, and knew what drugs Kennedy was taking.

Jacobson was outraged. Someone had violated the sanctity of not only his relationship with JFK, but also the relationships of all his patients. He remained silent as he prepared for his trip, though.

Before their flight took off, Jacobson received a call that the president wanted to see him before his departure on Air Force One. While Nina waited at the airport hotel, Jacobson went to the terminal where the president's plane was waiting. Before he reached the plane, he was intercepted by a large man who identified himself as a detective. The detective demanded to know Jacobson's identity.

According to Jacobson's diary (unpublished), the brief conversation went as follows: "I'm a doctor. And I have an appointment with President Kennedy."

The detective was highly suspicious. "You're coming with me."

In his most authoritarian tone, Jacobson replied, "If your future means anything to you, you had better take me to your supervisor who can identify me. The president's plane is already delayed by ten minutes."

The detective wasn't swayed, and he led a furious Jacobson down the corridor.

Fortunately for Jacobson, the detective's captain met them in the corridor, identified Jacobson on the spot, and confirmed his appointment with the president. By this time, a gaggle of curious reporters had converged, and the Secret Service had to form a blockade to keep them away from the president.

Once on board Air Force One, Jacobson explained that his lateness was due to an overanxious detective. Kennedy waved it off. He had bigger things on his mind. On the flight from D.C. to New York, he said, his back had given him trouble. He was worried and wanted Jacobson to prevent any complications that might arise during the long flight to Paris. The doctor gave the president another injection, left the plane, and made his way through the reporters surrounding the gate without answering any of their questions. When Jacobson and Nina boarded their plane, they soon realized they were the only passengers, and for the next six hours, they watched the flight attendants entertain themselves.

The Jacobsons arrived in Paris the following morning and were driven to the L'Hotel Napoleon, where they were to stay during the president's visit.

Jacobson was soon called to the Palais D'Orsay, the hotel reserved by the French government for visiting dignitaries, where he found the president's entourage in high spirits after President de Gaulle's dinner reception. When Jacobson saw Mrs. Kennedy, he noticed that she was very talkative and friendly, in contrast to her usually reserved behavior in Jacobson's presence, even when he was treating her with injections to relieve the pain of her migraines.

At the same time, he noticed an irregularity in an otherwise perfect molding in a corner of the room. He suspected a hidden camera and called Jackie's attention to it by pointing while putting a finger to his lips. She nodded in acknowledgment, and Jacobson made his way to the president's private room.

The president seemed very composed and greeted Max warmly, asking whether the Jacobsons had had an enjoyable flight. Then JFK became more serious and said, "I need to see you early in the morning."

Even in Paris, Max would later comment, the secret relationship between him and JFK had to be maintained. The next morning, he took a taxi to the Palais D'Orsay, and French soldiers allowed him to pass through to the floor where the president's private rooms were located. There he was stopped by the huissier, the head of the supervisory personnel at the Palais, who was ceremoniously dressed in an ornate cut-away uniform covered with ribbons and medals and wearing a huge sword at his side. "What are you doing here?" the huissier demanded.

"I have an appointment with the president," Jacobson told him. The huissier stared fixedly at the small attaché case the doctor carried in his left hand.

"What are you going to do there?" the huissier asked, never taking his eyes off the attaché case.

Jacobson answered, "I have been told that questions are only indiscreet if they are answered."

"Are you going to cut his hair?" the huissier asked.

"I could try that," Jacobson replied. "But I don't think I could do a good job."

The door to the room suddenly opened, and George, the president's valet, appeared in the doorway and said, "Doctor, the president is waiting for you."

Monsieur le Huissier retreated with apologies.

Jacobson administered Kennedy's morning injection, carefully noting the president's response. The dosage had to be accurate—not too much, or the president would appear as if he were in a stupor, nor too little, or the drug would not alleviate Kennedy's fatigue or stress. After the injection, Kennedy said that he wanted the Jacobsons to accompany him on Air Force One for the rest of the trip because he needed the doctor by his side at all times.

On the day of their departure to Vienna, the Secret Service arranged for Jacobson to sit in the front seat of one of the first cars in the president's motorcade. Jacobson heard a familiar voice from the backseat. It belonged to Dr. Janet Travell, the official White House physician, who resented Jacobson's presence, his proximity to the president, and the medications she was sure were harmful to the president. Her level of resentment was more than apparent. It had been obvious to him when they encountered each other in the corridors of the Palais D'Orsay and Travell had pointedly turned away to avoid acknowledging him. He knew it would be inappropriate to make a scene in public, so he told the driver he'd forgotten his raincoat at the Palais and jumped out of the car. He went directly to the Secret Service in charge of the motorcade. "I don't appreciate your sense of humor! Get me into another car," he demanded.

The route to the airport from the hotel was lined with cheering crowds. Kennedy, with all his youthful vigor, was a hero to not only the French, but also the new generation of people who had emerged from a war-torn Europe. What the Europeans didn't know about Kennedy's fragile condition didn't hurt them, but Jacobson was thrilled that he had been able to give the Europeans a reason to cheer.

At the airport, the Jacobsons were ushered aboard Air Force One. It was an honor to be placed close to the president's private quarters among many important dignitaries, not the least of which were secretary of state Dean Rusk and the president's military aides. It was a responsibility, too, because Jacobson knew that the president relied on having him and his medical kit close at hand whenever he felt at the end of his physical tether.

The tension aboard the plane gradually built as Air Force One circled Vienna and slowly made its approach. At the private debarkation point, the cabin doors opened, and the president deplaned, surrounded by his Secret Service detail, after which then the rest of the passengers were able to leave.

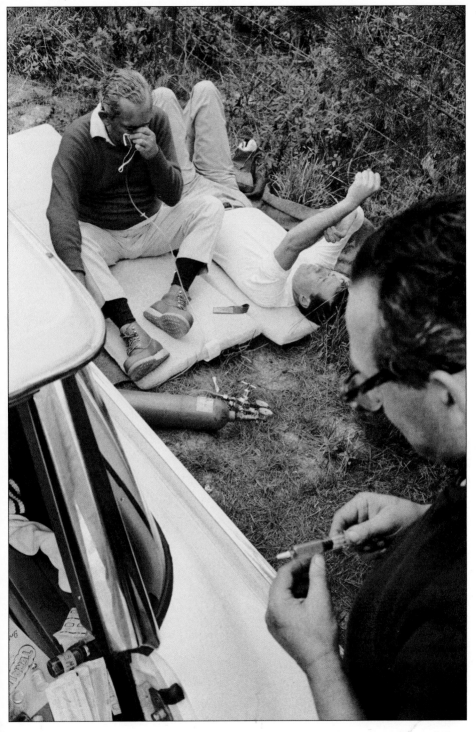

Dr. Max Jacobson prepares a syringe for JFK's friend Chuck Spalding while Prince Stash Radziwill (Lee Radziwill's husband and JFK's brother-in-law) rests during their fifty-mile hike with JFK in Florida. © Mark Shaw/ mptvimages.com

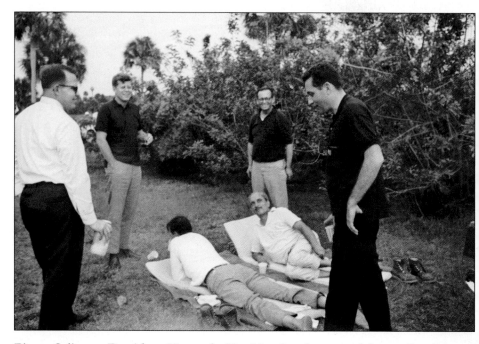

Pierre Salinger, President Kennedy, Dr. Max Jacobson, and Secret Service agent Clint Hill on the fifty-mile hike. On the ground are JFK's friend Chuck Spalding and Prince Stash Radziwill. © Mark Shaw/mptvimages.com

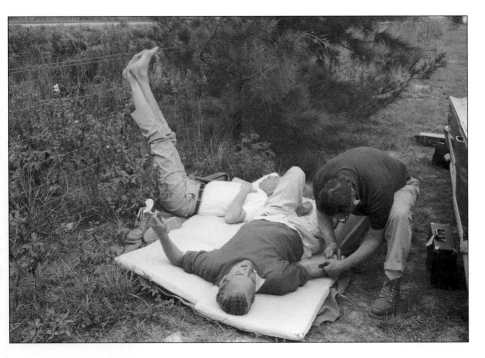

Max injecting Prince Stash Radziwill. Chuck Spalding is waiting for his injection. © Mark Shaw/mptvimages.com

Mark Shaw and Max Jacobson. © Mark Shaw/mptvimages.com

Max Jacobson in Boston in October 1967 while working with Alan Jay Lerner during the tryouts for *On a Clear Day You Can See Forever*. Photo courtesy of Alvin Aronson

Max in Hyannis.
Photo courtesy of C. David Heymann

Max receives a Medal of Freedom from Panama's Ambassador to the United Nations Eusebio Morales. Morales was a close friend and patient of Max Jacobson. He was also known as the "French Connection" and reputedly ran a drug ring out of Jacobson's office. Photo courtesy of C. David Heymann

Max in the lab with Prince Stash Radziwill. Photo courtesy of C. David Heymann

Vial of Max's formula, created by the McCann Erickson ad agency. Photo courtesy of C. Alvin Aronson

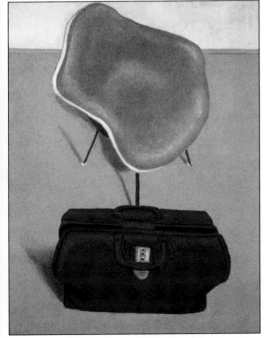

This painting was part of the Judy Jashinsky collection called *13 Days & 13 Nights: The Cuban Missle Crisis* that was shown at the National Gallery of Art in Washington, DC on October 26–December 1, 2012. This painting is called *Max Jacobson's (Dr. Feelgood) Medical Bag.* Photo courtesy of Judy Jashinsky

Max and Cecil B. DeMille. Photo courtesy of C. David Heymann

Max with Ingrid Bergman, Leonard Bernstein, Rosalind Russell, and Franco Zeffirelli. Photo courtesy of C. David Heymann

One of the last photographs taken of Max (with his wife Ruth and his grandchildren) shortly before his death in December 1979. Photo courtesy of C. David Heymann

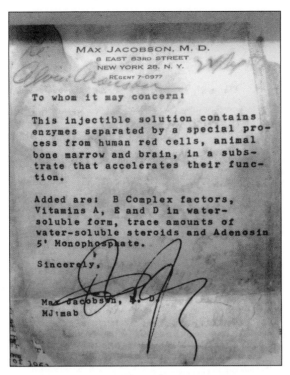

Max's prescription to Alvin Aronson.

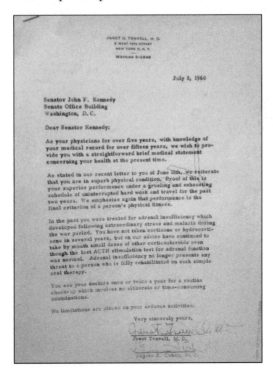

A letter from Dr. Travell to JFK stating a clean bill of health.
The letter was, of course, a lie.

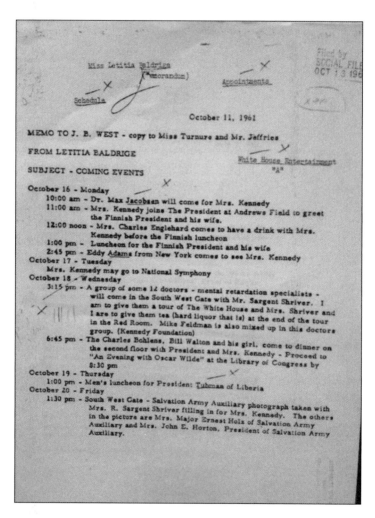

Filed by
SOCIAL FILE
OCT 13 196

Miss Letitia Baldrige
(Memorandum)

Schedule

Appointments

October 11, 1961

MEMO TO J. B. WEST - copy to Miss Turnure and Mr. Jeffries

FROM LETITIA BALDRIGE

SUBJECT - COMING EVENTS

White House Entertainment
"A"

October 16 - Monday
10:00 am - Dr. Max Jacobson will come for Mrs. Kennedy
11:00 am - Mrs. Kennedy joins The President at Andrews Field to greet the Finnish President and his wife.
12:00 noon - Mrs. Charles Englehard comes to have a drink with Mrs. Kennedy before the Finnish luncheon
1:00 pm - Luncheon for the Finnish President and his wife
2:45 pm - Eddy Adams from New York comes to see Mrs. Kennedy

October 17 - Tuesday
Mrs. Kennedy may go to National Symphony

October 18 - Wednesday
3:15 pm - A group of some 12 doctors - mental retardation specialists - will come in the South West Gate with Mr. Sargent Shriver. I am to give them a tour of The White House and Mrs. Shriver and I are to give them tea (hard liquor that is) at the end of the tour in the Red Room. Mike Feldman is also mixed up in this doctors group. (Kennedy Foundation)
6:45 pm - The Charles Bohlens, Bill Walton and his girl, come to dinner on the second floor with President and Mrs. Kennedy - Proceed to "An Evening with Oscar Wilde" at the Library of Congress by 8:30 pm

October 19 - Thursday
1:00 pm - Men's luncheon for President Tubman of Liberia

October 20 - Friday
1:30 pm - South West Gate - Salvation Army Auxiliary photograph taken with Mrs. R. Sargent Shriver filling in for Mrs. Kennedy. The others in the picture are Mrs. Major Ernest Holz of Salvation Army Auxiliary and Mrs. John E. Horton, President of Salvation Army Auxiliary.

Calendar of White House visitors with Max's name in it: "10:00 am - Dr. Max Jacobson will come for Mrs. Kennedy."

There were two motorcades carrying the Kennedy entourage from the airport. One motorcade followed Jacqueline Kennedy to her private engagement with Nina Khrushchev. Jackie was nervous about this but was prepared for delicate diplomacy. Jacobson's motorcade followed the president to the private residence of the American ambassador, a beautiful house in the Semmering, where the Summit meeting with Premier Khrushchev was to take place. The route to the mountains was lined with cheering crowds. There was hope in the atmosphere, and Max could feel it as the motorcade made its way through the American-flag-waving onlookers.

No sooner had the president's party arrived at the ambassador's residence when Jacobson was hurriedly ushered up to the president's room. Kennedy told him, "Khrushchev is supposed to be on his way over. The meeting may last for a long time. See to it that my back won't give me any trouble when I have to get up or move around." The doctor administered a heavy dose of methamphetamine to ease Kennedy's stress, give him energy, and build his confidence.

As it turned out, the president had been misinformed, and Khrushchev arrived much later, after the amphetamine began to wear off. Just before Khrushchev's arrival, JFK demanded another injection. Jacobson thought twice about it, but he could see the concern on the president's face and stuffed his professional feelings down. Although too many injections of amphetamines could have a deleterious effect, Jacobson told himself that this was the president of the United States, and the free world hung in the balance as Khrushchev's party assembled for the sit-down.

Jacobson waited in the wings, in case he needed to administer more injections. He passed the time looking out at the beautiful landscape of the Semmering Mountains and the large crowds of onlookers hoping to see the arriving dignitaries, the American president and the Soviet premier.

As the hours passed, Jacobson began to worry. Suddenly, the president appeared in the doorway. His face was sullen and fatigued, and he was clearly nervous.

"How are you feeling, Mr. President?" Jacobson asked him.

The president hesitated, then answered, "May I be at least permitted to pee first?" Kennedy's speech was slurred. When he returned, he asked for another shot. "I need it to get me through to the end. It's almost over. I need to feel good."

Jacobson demurred. "You've already had too much. Too much will cloud your thinking."

"But I need the edge," Kennedy said. "This guy's making all kinds of demands. He thinks he can push us around."

Reluctantly, Jacobson opened his attaché case. "This has to be the last time," he told the president. "No matter what happens, I can't let you have a serious overdose." And he gave President Kennedy one final injection of methamphetamine before sending him back to face Khrushchev.

A short time later, Kennedy came back to the anteroom where Jacobson waited. His complexion was brighter, even though he looked as though he'd been in a real fight. "Feeling fine," the president said. "You can go back to the hotel. We've finished here."

What Jacobson could not have known was just how badly the meeting had gone. In a private conversation with secretary of state Dean Rusk on the way back from the meeting, Kennedy tried to explain how Khrushchev had treated him like a weak and indecisive child, even though Kennedy had tried to be as accommodating as possible. It was the failure of the Bay of Pigs, at the very least, that might have showed Khrushchev that Kennedy was afraid to take him on. That, and Kennedy's performance, overdosed on a drug that Khrushchev knew all about because of the KGB raid on Dr. Jacobson's office, played directly into the Soviet premier's strategy to demand that the German reunification situation be settled within six months or else it would mean war. What would happen if the news leaked that the new president had been pushed around by Khrushchev? Whereas Eisenhower had stood up to the Russians even as he sought to avoid a nuclear war, Kennedy felt existentially threatened. Dean Rusk might have believed that despite all the preparation in advance of the summit, Kennedy was still underprepared. How much of his performance was the result of Max's multiple injections?

Just how despondent was Kennedy after the Vienna summit? While still at the ambassador's residence, Kennedy sat down for an interview with the *New York Times*'s correspondent James Reston. Kennedy was very frank when Reston asked him how things went. Kennedy's strategy, of course, was to get his version of the story out first so as to preempt any leaks from hostile journalists. He trusted Reston and wanted to convey just how menacing the situation was with the Soviets.

"He savaged me," Kennedy told Reston about Khrushchev. "It was the worst day of my life."

Kennedy went on to tell Reston that Khrushchev had "beaten the hell" out of him. What, of course, Kennedy did not reveal was that he had taken at least three injections of methamphetamine that day. And what Kennedy did not know was that because the KGB had raided Dr. Jacobson's office, it could be presumed that Khrushchev knew all about JFK's relationship with Jacobson and his reliance on the injections. What neither Kennedy nor Khrushchev knew was that the CIA was already aware of the raid from Mark

Shaw, the Kennedy family photographer, who was also former OSS and a CIA nonofficial cover officer. Shaw's identity as a CIA officer was confirmed by his children and by a former CIA nonofficial cover officer, who, for obvious reasons, will remain nameless.

Just how much difficulty the Kennedy Khrushchev meeting would create for the president soon became apparent within two months after the Vienna Summit, when the East Germans began construction on the Berlin Wall, thereby isolating the East German sector and creating a new set of tensions. And the following year, the Soviets would place ballistic missiles in Cuba, just ninety miles off the coast of Florida, posing not just a formidable challenge to the president but also demonstrating what happens when a president cannot hold his own in a room with Soviet adversaries. The CIA took special notice of how close the United States had come to a nuclear confrontation with the Soviet Union, something Kennedy's predecessor had so carefully and competently avoided.

In London, Kennedy was scheduled for meetings with British Prime Minister Harold McMillan to report on his summit with Khrushchev. It was crucial that the British understood the severity not only of Khrushchev's tone, but also his demands that implied that the Soviets would go to war over Germany. There were heavy war clouds gathering over Europe, perhaps precipitated by Kennedy's reluctance to send in American troops to support the invasion of Cuba at the Bay of Pigs. However, lurking in the background, unbeknownst to Max Jacobson, was Khrushchev's knowledge that the Soviets had what amounted to nothing less than an inside man, Jacobson himself, visiting the White House, who was doping the president of the United States. How much could that play into the Soviet strategy over the course of the ensuing year, and was Khrushchev already testing the resolve of the new president?

On JFK's arrival, the British crowds cheered the American president and his entourage, lining the streets along the way from Heathrow to central London, waving American flags just like the Viennese had. There were a few anti-nuke protestors holding posters, but their demands for a complete nuclear disarmament were drowned out by crowds welcoming the Kennedys.

Jacobson was looking forward to seeing his wife, who had proceeded to London ahead of him and was staying at Claridges near Hyde Park. Just as Max settled into their room at the Claridges, he received a summons to Number Four, Buckingham Palace, the home of JFK's brother-in-law, Prince Stanislaw Radziwill, for what he thought would be a simple meet and greet. It wasn't. Jacobson made sure to bring along his attaché case.

The car Kennedy sent took Jacobson to the back entrance of Buckingham Palace, where the driver escorted him through a garden to a door, which led through the employees' bathroom to a very steep staircase into a large foyer. From there, Max's driver led him up another staircase to the second floor where the bedrooms were located. He was ushered into Lee Radziwill's bedroom (Lee was Jackie's sister) where Jackie, the president, and Lee were simply chatting. President Kennedy motioned for Jacobson to follow him to an anteroom to administer another injection. Then he administered an injection to Jackie Kennedy, whom he had treated previously for migraines and depression in Washington and at the Kennedys's West Palm Beach. Having performed his duties, Jacobson retraced his steps out of the palace, where he was confronted by a tall, handsome, and elegantly dressed man who emerged from the shadows. He smiled at the elderly doctor, extended his hands, and said, "I am Lee's husband, Prince Radziwill. You can call me 'Stash.'" Prince Radziwill belonged to the Polish royal family. He and Jacobson were both Polish émigrés and both traveled in high circles. It would not be long before Stash Radziwill himself would become one of Max's patients as well as one of his friends.

The following day, the Jacobsons prepared for their flight home. Once on board, Jacobson immediately fell asleep, only to be awakened by a sharp poke in the ribs from Nina. When he opened his eyes, he saw President Kennedy in his nightshirt standing at the entrance of his private quarters.

"I need to talk to you, Max," the president said. "Could you come into my quarters?"

The summit was a strain, Kennedy said. And with all of the social activities, and the follow-up meetings, he knew that he was exhausted.

"My old back injury has been giving me discomfort," the president explained. "I want to thank you personally for helping me stay in control of it. I'm grateful." He said that the pain had never gotten in the way of his public appearances or meetings with heads of state. And with that, Max administered another injection to the president, was pleased that Kennedy said he felt very relaxed, left him in his quarters for his usual forty-five minute nap, and returned to the main cabin to find a discomfited Nina waiting for him.

Nina explained that while Jacobson was in the president's quarters, Eunice Shriver, the president's sister, had popped into the seat next to Nina and wanted to know what they were doing there on Air Force One.

"Ask my husband directly when he returns," Nina answered. But Eunice Shriver never followed up.

When the Jacobsons arrived in New York, they returned to their normal lives. It was too early to tell what the fallout from JFK's summit with Khrushchev might entail, but the young president's addiction to methamphetamines clearly gave the Soviet premier the advantage. Across an ocean and a continent, Khrushchev, believing that he held the key to controlling the president of the United States, made his plans for the Berlin Wall and for assembling the missiles he would place aboard ships for transport to Cuba. Kennedy's worst fears were about to come true, and they were coming true before the eyes of those deep inside the CIA, who already mistrusted him.

Chapter 8

Max, Mel, and "The Mick"

Mickey Charles Mantle remains one of the great American baseball legends of the twentieth century alongside Joe DiMaggio and Babe Ruth. He was a switch hitter who had great power with either hand and great overall athleticism that carried him from game to game in a long season. He also had charisma and swagger, key qualities not just for the Yankees but for a New York media market that fed on heroes. But like most heroes who are only human, the Mick had feet of clay. He drank excessively, socialized too much, and was a womanizer, a far cry from the wholesome, all-American boy he was portrayed as in the eyes of the public and adoring Yankee fans.

Well before he finally sought treatment for alcoholism at the Betty Ford Clinic in 1994, Mantle admitted his hard living had hurt both his playing and his family. His rationale was that the men in his family had all died young, so he expected to die young as well. His father had died of Hodgkin's disease at age forty in 1952, and his grandfather had also died young of the same disease. "I'm not gonna be cheated," he said on more than one occasion.

Mickey was not a choir boy in any way. He had cirrhosis of the liver from his alcoholism, he was called a "whore-monger" by sportscaster and Max Jacobson patient Howard Cosell, and even other ball players described Mantle's philandering while on the road. Others have called Mantle's lifestyle reckless and at times self-destructive. What would preclude him from extending his career with performance-enhancing drugs administered by Max Jacobson, especially if they were supposed to be a well-kept secret?

By 1961, when Mantle first met Dr. Jacobson, he was already a great New York Yankee legend. At almost thirty years old and at his peak, he had replaced the great Joe DiMaggio in the hearts and minds of Yankees fans. As a rookie, he had suffered from what was most likely a torn ACL, for which there was no treatment at the time, and he was still performing well mid-career. However, in 1961, during his homerun race with fellow Yankee Roger Maris, Mantle received a special injection from Dr. Jacobson, the first of many injections that ultimately led to his losing the homerun battle with his teammate.

According to Jacobson's friend Mike Samek, "Max prepared a special mixture for Mantle that included steroids, placenta, bone, calcium, and a very small amount of methamphetamine. I was there countless times when Mantle visited the office or received packages [of the mixture and syringes to self-inject]. Max spent a lot of time lecturing him not to drink. Max was very anti-alcohol and had a low tolerance for drinking. Max created his own version of steroids that was different from cortisone. I worked in the lab with him as he prepared the mixture."[28]

Samek's memory of Mantle as a longtime patient was confirmed by singer Eddie Fisher. "I saw Max treat Mantle many times in his office," he said. "I even saw Max give him a shot of cortisone at the airport when he complained to Max about his knee. . . . He was a patient, just as I was, who believed Max brought miracles. Dr. Needles. He was Miracle Max. He probably extended his [professional baseball] career. I'm not sure he got the meth like I did. He may have only got the cortisone. But who knows?"[29]

Actress Alice Ghostley's husband, actor Felice Orlandi, worked full time in Max's office for about eight years, during which Mantle was a frequent patient. "He was there quite a bit," Ghostley recalled, "as I remembered Felice always getting Yankee tickets from him." She believed that Felice delivered "packages" from Jacobson to Mantle. She did not know the content of the packages, but she could speculate about their contents. (April, 2006).

Jane Leavy, the author of the wonderfully researched book on Mantle, *The Last Boy: Mickey Mantle and the End of America's Childhood*, wrote in painstaking detail about a flawed Mantle. In her book, she reveals that on September 24, 1961, it was sportscaster Mel Allen, "the voice of the Yankees," who introduced Mantle to Jacobson. Mantle was in the final stretch of a legendary home run contest with Roger Maris to top Babe Ruth's 1927 home run record of sixty. Mantle had hit his fifty-fourth home run, but was feeling under the weather as his energy began to sputter. Maybe it was a virus, maybe a simple cold or an upper respiratory infection, that was hurting his game. When Mantle told Mel Allen how he was feeling, Allen said that he had a doctor who would give him a shot that would fix Mantle right up. Mantle agreed, and Allen made an appointment for Mantle to see Jacobson the following day.

Like President Kennedy, Leavy writes, "Mantle had a secret that required discreet medical intervention." Leavy says that according to what Mantle told his wife, "Dr. Max told Mantle to pull his pants down and filled the syringe with what Mantle later described as a smoky liquid. He squirted some into the air and plunged the needle deep into Mantle's hip. Too high, Mantle said later. It hit bone," he said.[30] This shot, possibly from a dirty needle, caused Mickey pain and a massive infection that resulted in hospitalization. He also missed the last few games of the season, which prevented him from breaking Babe Ruth's home run record, which Maris broke with sixty-one.

According to Leavy, Mantle "left the doctor's office in excruciating pain. The needle felt like a red-hot poker," she wrote. Jacobson advised him to play hurt. Walk it off. "Don't take a cab. You'll be fine." Leavy writes that Mantle's wife said that he "drug his leg all the way back to the hotel," and when she asked him what happened, he said, "I just got sucked dry by a vampire." She also told Leavy that "Mick told me, 'I think the guy wanted to hurt me.' And said his place was filthy and he had blood on his coat." Leavy also wrote that "Mantle said he never knew what was in Jacobson's syringe, and he never paid the bill, either."[31]

There are a few holes in Mantle's story as related by his wife to Leavy. First, with the thousands of injections that Jacobson had administered over his career, it is unlikely that he would have struck Mantle's hip bone. Second, Mantle was the toast of the town and Jacobson always treated such celebrities with great deference and care. It's unlikely that he would have been so cavalier to tell Mantle to "walk it off" when his objective was to make his patients feel better.

Another person who has described the relationship between Max Jacobson and Mickey Mantle is Curt Smith, one of baseball's leading historians and author of *The Voice: Mel Allen's Untold Story*. Smith's book corroborates Jane Leavy's account. He writes that Allen was not just a casual Jacobson patient, but a long-term patient who remained under Jacobson's care even after he was reportedly fired from the Yankees because of Mantle's reaction to Jacobson's shot. Allen continued to receive treatments even as he slipped further and further into a state of clinical depression. Curt Smith said that everyone thought that Mel Allen was simply an alcoholic, but he wasn't. Smith believed that it was the shots he was receiving that altered the announcer's behavior to the point where there were periods of dead air when Allen was announcing, word slurs, and simple mistakes about facts that a sportscaster shouldn't make. But Mel Allen never left Jacobson's care. In fact, Allen reportedly told Smith that Jacobson's shots "really worked."[32]

The late Ralph Houk, the former Yankee manager who took over the team in 1960, blamed Mel Allen directly for Mantle's turn to Jacobson in 1961. Once addicted, though, Mantle became a regular patient, and although he would never approach overturning Babe Ruth's record again, his career in baseball continued. He kept on playing, even through the pains in his legs and his torn ACL, until the end of the 1968 baseball season. He retired in March 1969.

Mickey Mantle was a sophisticated sports celebrity as he got older and more comfortable with his fame. He was not adverse to taking stimulants, as Jim Bouton's classic book *Ball Four*[33] later revealed. Greenies (stimulants, also called "uppers") were prevalent in the clubhouse. *Cleveland Plain Dealer* sports columnist Terry Pluto wrote that, "I do know that in 1961, Kubek and the others thought Mantle was getting a cortisone shot—Ray Miller told me that he took cort shots 15–20 times one season in AAA . . . As for what Mantle took, no idea. I do know about the Yankees in 1961 . . . I wrote about it in a book with Tony Kubek.[34] Back then, players drank a lot and did a lot of greenies. That's all I know."[35] If what Terry Pluto says is true, Mantle would certainly have been aware of performance-enhancing drugs.

The lingering question is whether Mick's records should be altered to reflect that he was taking performance-enhancing drugs, steroids, and methamphetamines. If Barry Bonds, Mark McGwire, and Sammy Sosa's records record their use of performance-enhancing substances, should not Mantle's? Especially in the wake of stories of Lance Armstrong's use of drugs and his confession to television personality Oprah Winfrey, sports fans have become more conscious of the effect that steroids and other substances can have on a user's performance. Is Mickey Mantle immune from the same kind of scrutiny?

Mickey Mantle was indeed an American legend. Like President Kennedy, he was a hero for an entire generation, even though that public perception of heroism tends, sometimes, to obscure real facts about the human being himself. Also, just like President Kennedy, Mickey Mantle was a victim of a powerfully addictive drug that held out the promise of superhuman energy, but in the end sapped the very energy it was intended to enhance.

Chapter 9
Marilyn

Screen legend Marilyn Monroe had a very troubled childhood, sought father figures throughout her life, and had numerous affairs with the men who guided her career. She died in her Brentwood home in 1962 under what Los Angeles coroner Dr. Thomas Noguchi said were suspicious circumstances. Had she committed suicide by overdosing on chloral hydrate and Nembutal, despondent over her failed love affairs with president John F. Kennedy and his brother, attorney general Robert F. Kennedy, or her failed marriages to New York Yankee slugger Joe DiMaggio and playwright Arthur Miller? Or had she been murdered, or, rather, "suicided" by mysterious agents of the government because she was an embarrassment to the Kennedys and simply knew too much? And what was that strange bruise on her hip, noted by Dr. Noguchi, indicating that she might have been bleeding subcutaneously shortly before her death? What was known for certain was that Monroe had been one of Dr. Max Jacobson's regular patients, kept stimulated by regular injections of methamphetamines that Jacobson supplied to her friends in Frank Sinatra's celebrated Rat Pack.

We know from stories told about Jacobson that he not only had an affinity for famous and powerful people, but he also was fascinated by beautiful women and said so himself. Jacobson was obsessed with control—control of others exerted by his distribution of the pathogenically addictive methamphetamine he supplied. He used his drugs to entice high-profile, fashionable women into his "harem." He had already hooked Marlene Dietrich, Elizabeth Taylor, Judy Garland, Ingrid Bergman, Hedy Lamarr, Arlene Francis, Rosemary Clooney, and countless other admired women of that generation and was hoping to add Marilyn Monroe to the top of his list.

By the 1950s, Monroe was already an iconic film star and had surpassed her idol Betty Grable when she took up residence in a three-room suite at the Waldorf-Astoria in New York City. She had married, and then divorced, Yankee baseball star Joe DiMaggio. In New York, she soon became fast friends with Truman Capote.

Capote claimed he made two important introductions for Monroe. The first was to Cheryl Crawford, who was one of the founders of the Actors Studio. Marilyn had already met Paula Strasberg and her daughter, Susan, on the set of *There's No Business Like Show Business*. Marilyn was a great admirer of Lee Strasberg, the director of the Actor's Studio, and wanted to study with him. Crawford introduced Monroe to Strasberg, and she began taking private lessons with him. Although Marilyn was already an iconic American movie star, she soon entered a class with such beginners as Julie Newmar and Jane Fonda. There were also several young actors at the Actor's Studio during this period, including Marlon Brando, James Dean, Montgomery Clift, Julie Harris, Martin Landau, Dennis Hopper, Patricia Neal, Paul Newman, Eli Wallach, Ben Gazzara, Rip Torn,

Kim Stanley, Anne Bancroft, Shelley Winters, Sidney Poitier, Joanne Woodward, and others. It was as if Marilyn had entered into a future pantheon of some of America's greatest actors.

In his *Vanity Fair* article, "Marilyn and Her Monsters,"[36] Sam Kashner wrote:

> Monroe was also encouraged by Strasberg to be treated by Dr. Margaret Hohenberg as often as five times a week. . . . The psychiatrist, an acquaintance of Strasberg's, was a Brünnhilde type, a fifty-seven-year-old Hungarian immigrant complete with tightly wound braids and a Valkyrian bosom. Strasberg strongly believed that Monroe needed to open up her unconscious and root through her troubled childhood, all in the service of her art. Between her sessions with Strasberg and with Dr. Hohenberg, she began recording some of those raked-up memories, including a devastating incident of sexual abuse.

It was during this period that Capote introduced Marilyn to Dr. Max Jacobson, who had been lobbying Capote to bring his new friend to his office. While Monroe's psychological well-being was being treated by Dr. Hohenberg, Capote told her how Jacobson's vitamin shots could help her with her lack of energy, as they had with his writer's block.

Another version of the Marilyn-to-Jacobson story was told by singer Marian Marlowe, from the old *Arthur Godfrey* television show. She and Marilyn had been roommates as early as 1954, and she said that she had brought the young actress to visit Max Jacobson even before Marilyn married Arthur Miller and met Truman Capote. Either way, whether in 1954 or in 1956, Marilyn became Dr. Max

Jacobson's patient and became addicted to his methamphetamine injections.

By 1956, Monroe had come under the control of what amounted to four Svengalis—Strasberg, Hohenberg, Jacobson, and her new husband, Arthur Miller. Each fought for control over her professional and personal life. Strasberg sought the spiritual, Hohenberg wanted the mind, Jacobson sought her soul, and Miller wanted her allegiance. For a woman who had unresolved father and authority issues, Marilyn was constantly in a state of conflict. Her search for a father figure played out again and again in her relationships with men and those in authority. Accordingly, it makes perfect sense that Monroe would have responded to Max Jacobson, a domineering figure whose magic elixir could bestow on her the ability to feel good, physically and emotionally.

Jacobson, however, was not a benevolent father figure. He was angry with Monroe not only because of her drinking, but also because he suspected that she took barbiturates while she was on amphetamines. He told his patients that if they drank or took barbiturates, he could not be responsible for them because of the cross-reactions between methamphetamines and other mood-altering substances. Yet he was not so quickly dismissive of Monroe because he considered her a conquest, and Jacobson wanted her dependent on him.

Monroe was an infrequent visitor to Jacobson's renowned after-hour office gatherings of his literary and artistic patients. While there is no record of whether Arthur Miller attended these get-togethers, other artists certainly did, such as Tennessee Williams, Alan Jay Lerner, Carson McCuller, Zero Mostel, Leonard Bernstein, and Gypsy Rose Lee. There was always a specially prepared syringe of Jacobson's special vitamin stimulant cocktail loaded with meth for those who stayed after three o'clock in the morning.

When Monroe returned to Los Angeles to shoot *Bus Stop* and *Some Like It Hot*, she received her medications from Max's son, Dr. Thomas Jacobson, who was then a successful physician in Los Angeles.

Of those early days, Dr. Tommy Jacobson recalled, "I was separate from my father; however, I began to treat several of his patients who were in Los Angeles, such as [Eddie] Fisher and Monroe. There were times that my father sent his prepared mixtures to be administered to them. My father called his mixture 'miracle tissue regeneration.'"[37] In reality the mixture was a blend of amphetamines, vitamins, painkillers, steroids, and human placenta. These ingredients were itemized in a Freedom of Information Act document that resulted from Bobby Kennedy's test of Jacobson's formula by the Drug Enforcement Administration and a later report by the Bureau of Narcotic and Dangerous Drugs.

By the early 1960s, Monroe was under the constant care of a new psychiatrist named Dr. Ralph Greenson. She was struggling with depression and with drug and alcohol dependency. Despite the critical success of Billy Wilder's *Some Like It Hot*, according to actor Tony Curtis, with whom she had an affair during this period, she was still suffering.

After the grueling production of the film *The Misfits*, in which Monroe starred with Clark Gable and Montgomery Clift, and which Arthur Miller had written for her, she separated from Miller. Marilyn had troubles on the set; she was often late, difficult to work with, and unpredictable in her behavior because she resisted John Huston's direction of the film. She returned to New York in March 1961, and the world came crashing down around her. She committed herself to the Payne-Whitney psychiatric ward at the New York

Hospital. It was a horrible, confining experience that lasted three days, until ex-husband Joe DiMaggio rescued her. She returned to Los Angeles and continued receiving her treatments from Jacobson through his son. But her life was about to take another dramatic turn when her friend, actor Peter Lawford, invited her to his broth-er-in-law's birthday party, saying that he wanted to introduce her to his brother-in-law, who was turning forty-five.

Lawford's brother-in-law was none other than President John F. Kennedy, and the party would be a star-studded Democratic Party fundraising event at Madison Square Garden televised before a national audience on May 19, 1962. The "Who's Who" of show business would be there to pay homage to Kennedy. Among them were singers Harry Belafonte, Ella Fitzgerald, and Peggy Lee, comedian Jack Benny, actor Henry Fonda, and opera diva Maria Callas. Lawford, who was to serve as the master of ceremonies, wanted Monroe to perform the pièce de résistance by singing the finale.

When Jackie Kennedy learned that Monroe would perform, she became a last-minute participant in the Loudoun Hunt Horse Show at Glen Ora, her weekend home. Jackie knew her husband's propensity for beautiful women, and that he was fascinated with Marilyn Monroe, and she was not about to be humiliated in front of a national audience.

Monroe was wild for Kennedy, too, and she accepted the invitation, even though it was in violation of her performance contract with Twentieth Century Fox. Marilyn was in a narcotics and booze nosedive and living on impulse. She was in hot pursuit of Jack Kennedy, and nothing would get in her way. "A manic energy propelled her," wrote Barbara Leaming in *Marilyn Monroe*.[38] "All weekend, the white-carpeted, unfurnished rooms at Fifth Helena [Monroe's home in Los Angeles] echoed with Marilyn's whispery voice. She lay in the tub singing 'Happy Birthday.' She sat on the living room floor, endlessly tape-recording and listening to herself."

Ignoring her studio's stern warning, Monroe flew from Hollywood to New York with Peter Lawford. She continued to practice the song in her New York apartment. Those who listened said that her interpretation grew sexier and more and more outrageous. Friend Paula Strasberg warned that her performance was verging on self-parody.

On the night of party, Monroe got into her flesh-toned slip of a dress by Jean-Louis. The gown was so snug that she literally had to be sewn into it. Suddenly, she became paralyzed with stage fright. Monroe was never a stage actress and had very little experience performing live. Fortunately, Dr. Max Jacobson was there with his medical bag. Mike Samek was backstage with Jacobson, and witnessed his exchanges with Kennedy and Monroe:

> I had followed Max backstage to meet with the president . . . .
> I stood by as Max prepared a syringe and injected the president. We turned around and saw Marilyn Monroe behind us, and she was absolutely shivering. She saw Max and smiled. Without saying one word, Max went into his bag, prepared another syringe, and injected Monroe in the neck. She gave Max a peck on the cheek, and we went back to our wives and our seats.[39]

At first Monroe ignored her cue to appear on stage, waiting for Max's injection to take effect. Then Milt Ebbins shoved her onto the stage, and Jacobson remembered, "She walked like a geisha." The 15,000 people in Madison Square Garden that night couldn't believe what they were seeing. As Sally Bedell Smith describes in her book *Grace and Power: The Private World of the Kennedy White House,* [40] "Onto the stage sashayed Marilyn Monroe, attired in a great bundle of white mink. Arriving at the lectern, she turned and swept the furs from her shoulders. A slight gasp rose from the audience before it was realized that she was really wearing a skintight, flesh-toned gown." Hugh Sidey of *Time* magazine noted, "When she came down in that flesh-colored dress, without any underwear on, you could just smell lust. I mean, Kennedy went limp or something. We all were just stunned to see this woman. 'What an ass . . . what an ass,' whispered Kennedy."[41]

Monroe began to sing in a hushed voice, sometimes barely above a whisper, "Happy . . . Birthday . . . to you." She was soft, seductive, under the influence of Max's powerful drugs, as she desperately reached out across the audience for the love of just one man. The wig she was wearing was slipping off, and her eyes had a dreamy quality as she looked at the president. Some called it a brilliant performance. Others thought it was pathetic. Columnist Dorothy Kilgallen at the time suggested that it looked like Marilyn was "making love" to JFK in front of a viewing audience of forty million Americans.[42]

Afterward, President Kennedy spoke to the audience. He was noticeably embarrassed and announced disingenuously, "I can now retire from politics after having had Happy Birthday sung to me in such a sweet, wholesome way." It was clear that Marilyn and the president were more than just passing friends.

During the last months of Monroe's life, she was passed from JFK to his brother Bobby and watched over by Peter Lawford while the CIA was tapping her phone. By the beginning of August 1962, however, her affair had soured. Both Kennedys had broken up with her, and she became angry and out of control. According to an authenticated CIA transcript of a CIA wiretap, Monroe left a phone message for Bobby Kennedy on August 3, 1962, demanding to speak to Jack Kennedy and threatening to reveal her affair with the president, classified intelligence regarding bases in Cuba, the president's plans to kill Castro, and the president's revelation of a secret air base where he saw artifacts from outer space. Columnist Dorothy Kilgallen speculated that Monroe was referring to the Roswell incident and that this could be a huge embarrassment for him. Worse, the existence of the Nevada airbase, now referred to as Area 51, was beyond top secret. Clearly, the president had been pillow talking out of school.

The contents of the phone message apparently panicked members of the CIA team assigned to keep watch over Monroe. Kennedy had engaged in hushed out-of-schooltalk with his mistress, revealing classified information he had had sworn to keep secret. Leaks had to be plugged. Three days later, Monroe was dead, but Jacobson's treatment of Jack Kennedy continued as the president, himself becoming out of control, lurched forward to his next crisis: Vietnam.

Chapter 10

Dallas

Marilyn was dead, but the incipient Vietnam War was alive, too alive, and threatening to get worse. If Marilyn had gotten out of control, turning a simple sexual encounter—not the only one for the president—into a budding romance that not even being passed off to Bobby Kennedy could satisfy, then it was good that she was gone, at least according to Kennedy brother-in-law Peter Lawford. The president had become more reliant on Max Jacobson's injections despite continued warnings from his doctor, Janet Travell, who urged him to discontinue the treatments. She didn't trust Jacobson because she believed that what Jacobson was injecting into the president was harmful and explained on many occasions that the painkillers and steroid therapy she prescribed were conflicting with the drugs Jacobson was administering. By this time, Dr. Travell would have known about the contents of Jacobson's injections and known that methamphetamines, topical anesthetics like Provocaine, and steroids could create dangerous physical and psychological side effects. Moreover, simply the constant presence of the strange doctor with a thick German accent hanging around the president was unnerving. The press had also taken notice of Max Jacobson, who carried a thick black medical bag and followed the Kennedy family from Washington, to Massachusetts, and to Florida. Was the president really suffering from an incurable disease?

By December 1962, JFK's worries about the press's attention to his medical issues were bubbling up. The press had begun to sniff around all the doctors that were going in and out of the White House. If word leaked out that Kennedy was dependent on drugs that might alter his perception or his personality, what would that tell the public about the man who had his finger on the nuclear trigger? In the wake of the disaster in Vienna and the October Cuban Missile Crisis, those around JFK who knew about his medical condition and his reliance on Jacobson were also worried. The last thing the Kennedy inner circle wanted was to have to face questions about the president's medical condition as the machinery for the 1964 reelection campaign was beginning to ramp up.

Kennedy friends and supporters in the White House told secretary Evelyn Lincoln that if Dr. Janet Travell was going to keep making innuendos concerning the president's health, she would lose the support of his friends. Dr. Eugene Cohen, another one of Kennedy's medical advisors, suggested to him that Travell was a possible threat to Kennedy's condition because of the constant painkiller injections she was giving him. Kennedy agreed with Cohen and turned the management of his back injuries over to other doctors, but kept Travell on as the White House physician because he was afraid that if he fired her, she would leak stories about his physical condition to the press. But Bobby Kennedy wasn't satisfied with any of this. In early 1962, Bobby Kennedy had asked Jacobson for a sample of the medicine he was administering to the president. He secured fifteen vials of the drugs from his brother's own stash and another five directly from Jacobson to make sure the medicines were identical. Bobby turned all of these samples over to the FBI laboratory for analysis. When the results came back that Jacobson had formulated a substance with significant amounts of amphetamines, at least thirty milligrams, Bobby confronted his brother about it. JFK was blunt, telling Bobby that the ingredients were inconsequential to him—"I don't care if it's horse piss. . . . It makes me feel good," JFK said, according to Mike Samek.[43]

Jacobson continued to visit the White House, often flown to Washington by his patient Mark Shaw, the Kennedy family photographer, or Mike Samek. In April 1962 Bobby confronted Jacobson and his friend Samek in the White House. According to Samek, Bobby said, "What are you fuckin' kikes doing in the White House? You Jews aren't welcome here. Go back to New York with the other Jews."[44]

Jacobson was incensed. To him, this was a case of "been there, heard that." He was not going to go through this again, not in this country, not after the Holocaust, not in 1962 as the Civil Rights Movement was heating up. Jacobson later sent a letter to JFK via the president's secretary, Evelyn Lincoln, explaining that he wouldn't be visiting the White House or treating the president anymore, not after that personal insult. But JFK was desperate; he needed Jacobson because he was so dependent on the doctor's injections. Kennedy probably never realized that Jacobson, too, was needy for control, needy to bask in the glory of the White House. In fact, Kennedy probably never knew that Jacobson needed him more than he needed Jacobson. He relied on those injections and had to make up with Max no matter what his brother had said. He flew to New York, took a suite at the Carlyle Hotel, and asked Jacobson to meet him there.

When Jacobson arrived, carrying the special medical bag that Mike Samek had designed for him, he was ushered up to Kennedy's suite, where he immediately prepared the president's injection. While it took effect, he made his peace with the president, who implored him to overlook what his brother Bobby had said. JFK prevailed on Jacobson to keep treating him, at the very least for the good of his adopted country, the country that had became his haven from the Nazis. Jacobson acquiesced. Kennedy also begged the doctor to move into the White House so he could always be on hand. Jacobson demurred, telling Kennedy that he couldn't give up his New York practice, especially his work with neuromuscular disease patients, because many of them had nowhere to turn. They agreed that Jacobson would come to the White House whenever he was needed. For the record, Jacobson's name turns up more than thirty times in the official White House visitor logs, according to Seymour Hersh, who wrote *The Dark Side of Camelot*. Records also show that Max Jacobson was injecting patients, including JFK, who also self-injected, with concoctions containing more than thirty milligrams of methamphetamine, a huge dose of the stimulant that, on the downside rebound, was capable of causing all kinds of psychotic reactions.

Jacobson had indeed overdosed the president. After he left the Carlyle, the president, who at first felt invigorated and vibrant, suddenly began suffering from a serious psychotic reaction to the drugs and became manic. It was an absolute psychotic break. He peeled off all of his clothing and began prancing around his hotel suite. If his Secret Service detail was amused at first, they became worried when the president left the suite and began roaming through the corridor of the Carlyle. With press photographers downstairs in the lobby, the president could become easily compromised. And what made matters even worse was that JFK had another agenda for coming to New York. He had a habit of slipping away from his Secret Service detail to visit women with whom he had made arrangements in advance for sexual encounters. If Kennedy was in danger of becoming compromised by running naked through the halls of a hotel, imagine what might have happened if he became compromised by a KGB agent planted in New York to woo him away from the Secret Service. This was an untenable situation.

For the immediate moment in the Carlyle, one can only imagine how consternation turned to worry and ultimately turned to panic among JFK's staff as he left his suite at the Carlyle, delusional as he was under the influence of a megadose of methamphetamines from Dr. Max, and began to roam the corridors. He was completely naked, on the verge of paranoia, and feeling so free of pain that he almost performed gymnastic acts in the hallway. The Secret Service detail had to control him, but can you put a president in a straightjacket? Even his military liaison, the officer who handled the nuclear ICBM codes, and, most of all, intelligence operatives serving in the White House, knew this was a completely unacceptable situation. Therefore, the issue now facing the Kennedy entourage was how to get the president under control, sedated, back into the suite, and back to normal. They needed a doctor, and fast.

An emergency telephone call went out to one of New York City's most respected psychiatrists, Dr. Lawrence Hatterer. Dr. Hatterer explained that when he received the call of an utmost emergency at the Carlyle regarding the medical condition of the president of the United States, he immediately rushed across town to offer treatment. Dr. Hatterer said that he saw the president in a manic condition furiously waving his arms and running around without any clothes on. No one knew what to do. Hatterer instantly recognized a drug-induced mania. He opened his medical satchel, withdrew a vial of chlorpromazine, an antipsychotic and dopamine antagonistic drug, and injected the now-restrained president and monitored his condition as the drugs took effect and JFK's mania subsided. Kennedy slowly returned to his senses. There was no need to call vice president Lyndon Johnson, who already knew about JFK's physical and mental condition from his friend in the United States Senate, Richard Nixon.

Other eyes were on the president as well, ever-vigilant eyes that were not as benevolent as those of Kennedy's own staff or members of the Secret Service. These eyes had read the FBI file on Max Jacobson, his dealings with Communist sympathizers and possible Soviet agents, and his treatments of pro-socialist artists and celebrities as well as his treatment of CIA nonofficial cover officer Mark Shaw. These eyes had borne witness to the debacles in Cuba and Vienna when the president had told James Reston of the *New York Times* that he had experienced the worst day of his life in his meeting with Nikita Khrushchev. And now the president was demonstrating his inability to control himself while on serious stimulant drugs. Was this a president who could complete a second term? Was this a president who should be allowed to complete his first?

For all of his popularity with the American public, this was a president, who, under the influence of stimulants, was lining up assignations with disreputable women at locations that could not be guarded. What if one of these women was a KGB agent? Hadn't Kennedy already revealed state secrets to Marilyn Monroe?

Kennedy had already crossed the CIA, particularly the director Allen Dulles, when he refused to reinforce the Bay of Pigs invasion of Cuba to overthrow Fidel Castro. Dulles was not a person to take that kind of double-crossing lightly. Soon there would come another slight to the CIA that would threaten to reduce its influence in the intelligence community significantly, and it came in the form of secret Senate subcommittee testimony. In April 1962, a then relatively obscure Army lieutenant colonel named Philip J. Corso, who was working as the director of the Army Office of Research and Development's Foreign Technology Division and who had served on President Eisenhower's national security staff as well as on General Douglas MacArthur's staff during the Korean War, testified before the Senate's Internal Government Security Subcommittee that the CIA was laundering money for drug growers in Southeast Asia, Thailand, Cambodia, and Vietnam. This was a source of untraceable money, he said, for the CIA to support its black operations. In addition, Corso testified, the CIA was doctoring its National Intelligence Estimates to be more favorable to the Soviet Union. And Corso, who had tactical nuclear weapons under his control in Germany when he commanded an anti-aircraft missile battalion, had lots of credibility. Corso's testimony was classified, but its transcript soon found its way to attorney general Robert Kennedy.

The attorney general asked Corso and the committee if he could read Corso's testimony. Corso said that Robert Kennedy could read the testimony if, and only if, he promised to hand that testimony over to the president. This was how JFK learned that the CIA was engaging in narcotics trafficking in Southeast Asia. President Kennedy, who felt that a war in Southeast Asia would undermine his domestic agenda, ultimately ordered the dissolution of the CIA paramilitary, while at the same time facilitating the creation of the United States Army Special Forces and Navy SEALs. It would be a direct blow to the reach and power of the CIA. But the CIA had a card to play in the person of vice president Lyndon B. Johnson, the former leader of the Senate, who was becoming implicated in the Bobby Baker and Billy Sol Estes scandals, and who could just as easily find himself under the threat of indictment and off the 1964 Democratic national ticket. Would this be like a game of Monopoly: Go directly to jail, or go to the White House and collect your $200? LBJ had been a player. He would understand. And his hatred of the Kennedys would drive the day for the CIA if it needed him.

Then in October 1962, Nikita Khrushchev decided to play his hand. He had wanted the United States to remove its guided missiles from Turkey, missiles that were already obsolete but nevertheless posed a threat. Khrushchev dropped the nuke card by installing guided missiles in Cuba less than one hundred miles off the coast of the US mainland. He believed that Kennedy, frightened at Soviet blustering and compromised by drugs, would simply turn the other way and do nothing.

According to Army Lieutenant Colonel Philip Corso, Kennedy at first ignored the images he received from the National Reconnaissance Office that indicated the construction of a missile launch site in Cuba as well as the missiles themselves. But soon newspaper reporters picked up the story, leaked by intelligence community insiders, and the president's hand was forced. This would become a major crisis when Kennedy made his demand that the Soviets withdraw the missiles. General Curtis LeMay, a former commander of the Strategic Air Command who had been instrumental in developing the United States satellite surveillance capability, advocated the strategic bombing of Cuban missile sites and a subsequent invasion of Cuba. Kennedy, however, ordered a naval blockade of the island, relying on his instincts that Khrushchev would think twice about starting a war in US home waters.

Meanwhile, as the Kennedy inner circle and Pentagon command fretted over what the Soviet reaction would be, the U.S. Air Force prepared for the possible bombing of North America by alerting its interceptor squadrons to fly to their failsafe points off the coast of Alaska to await the Soviet bomber fleet. These fighters were equipped with nuclear air-to-air missiles, and they were flying over US territory. This was a deadly serious game and one of the closest moments the United States would ever come to a nuclear war. Kennedy was about to undo all that Ike had accomplished during his eight years in office trying to defuse the nuclear threat. And the CIA watched in horror.

It was a president on drugs, out of control, and through his own inexperience, ineptitude, and psychological vulnerabilities, bringing the United States to the brink of a nuclear war. Something had to be done before a catastrophe occurred and things ended up very badly. What card could the CIA play?

After Kennedy agreed to remove US missiles from Turkey, thereby placating Khrushchev by offering a face-saving way out of the situation, Air Force Chief of Staff General Curtis LeMay still advocated for an invasion of Cuba. But Kennedy refused. Kennedy then made plans to withdraw American military advisors from Vietnam, which included the CIA's own personnel. Now the US military was concerned as well because, in addition to seeing Vietnam as a bulwark against the spread of Communism, the military saw that JFK was taking the United States out of contention for possession of the valuable deepwater port of Haiphong in North Vietnam, a port vital to oil tankers transporting oil from drilling operations in the South China Sea. All of this might have been tangential to Kennedy's addiction to Jacobson's methamphetamines, but the results were cumulative. The CIA and the military now had similar issues at stake while the young president, under the influence of drugs, was in multiple compromising sexual affairs.

During the last year of the Eisenhower administration, as the CIA planned for the invasion of Cuba, it had forged links in south Florida with local organized crime capos with ties to the Cuban expatriate community. The crime cartels, which had been instrumental in helping the United States Army and its intelligence command infiltrate and conquer Sicily in World War II, had sought to exert their influence in Cuba as Castro's forces assembled in the mountains. Indeed, crime boss Lucky Luciano had moved to Cuba in 1956 to establish himself as the gambling czar, but President Eisenhower had demanded that he leave. The CIA kept in close contact with Luciano as well as organized crime bosses Santos Trafficante and Carlos Marcello. The CIA urged Kennedy to order the assassination of Fidel Castro using mob-controlled hit men, which Marilyn Monroe had referred to in her threatening message to Bobby Kennedy, and in the wake of the Bay of Pigs disaster, Kennedy had given them the green light. The CIA forged additional links with local organized crime bosses, including Sam "Momo" Giancana, who had negotiated with JFK's father, Joseph Kennedy, Sr., for the delivery of the Cook County, Illinois, vote. Joe Kennedy had promised Giancana that his sons would leave the mob cartels alone, but Bobby Kennedy, as attorney general, refused to play along, and held Senate hearings on mob infiltration of legitimate businesses. And President Kennedy, it was clear, had blabbed highly confidential information to his mistress. This information flow had to stop.

Removing an out-of-control and potentially self-destructive head of state was no easy task; however, it had been attempted in recent history, according to Bert E. Park, M.D., in World War II. Adolf Hitler had a doctor, Theodore Morell, on whom Max Jacobson might have modeled his experiments with methamphetamines. Morell injected Hitler as well as Eva Braun with high doses of liquid methamphetamines. These doses, in the thirty to forty milligram range, distorted Hitler's perception and increased his feelings of paranoia and grandiosity. Hitler's delusions of self-grandeur, his frequent psychotic breaks, and his decision to invade the Soviet Union, which resulted in the collapse of the Wehrmacht on the Eastern Front, so alarmed his general staff that they plotted his assassination. Led by Claus von Stauffenberg, the generals plotted to blow up a conference led by Hitler in July 1944. But the plot failed. This famous episode almost a year before the Allied capture of Berlin and the German surrender was well-known in American intelligence circles.

None of this should be construed as a comparison of JFK to Hitler. It is simply an illustration of what can happen when a powerful leader is clearly having psychotic reactions to methamphetamines. JFK was not only receiving injections of thirty to forty milligrams of methamphetamines from Dr. Jacobson, but also was self-injecting huge doses on top of the painkillers Dr. Janet Travell was administering.

Admiral George Burkley, the doctor who would sign Kennedy's death certificate, forced Travell out of the White House because he believed that she was giving the president too many injections of Provocaine. Burkley also wanted Jacobson banned from the White House because he understood the devastating effects of methamphetamine, especially the types of psychotic reactions, hypersexuality, hypergrandiose paranoia, and chemical addiction that came with it, but JFK persisted and continued to receive treatments from

Jacobson.

In addition to these injections, President Kennedy was also taking marijuana and LSD, which Army Intelligence had used as a form of mind control as early as the 1950s. LSD, because it was first developed by doctors for the purposes of curing addictive behavior such as alcoholism, might have been effective in weaning the president off Max Jacobson's meth injections, some CIA operatives believed. But it only seemed to exacerbate Kennedy's drug dependency and libido. Either the president's drug addiction or Addison's disease was likely to prove fatal in the end. CIA operatives saw real danger on the horizon.

The question confronting the CIA was what to do. CIA director Allen Dulles was already an enemy of the White House. With the CIA officially out of Vietnam, there was no more funding from narcotraffickers. What assets could the CIA muster?

Looking at the groups forming a critical mass of not just opposing where the Kennedy administration was going, but actually seeking revenge against the president, the CIA could have been looking for someone to hold this unholy, soon-to-be alliance together. And that someone was vice president Lyndon Johnson, who hated the Kennedy clan as much as anyone, felt that he had been overwhelmed by Kennedy money during the Democratic primary, and chafed at being a vice president with a civil rights agenda he wanted to pursue and no way to put it into action. LBJ was likely to be pushed off the ticket by Bobby Kennedy, and possibly put under federal investigation for corruption or racketeering. Then there was J. Edgar Hoover, a power-hungry bureaucrat with his own skeletons in the closet. He hated the CIA because he believed they trampled all over his turf, but, as a Washington insider who had kept his grip on power ever since the Palmer Raids in 1924, he knew when to go along.

Like most aspects of a well-concealed homicide, evidence lurks in the corners, usually in plain sight, but almost always is overlooked, except by those who know where the corners are. For example, why would Max Jacobson's name come up at all if the CIA hadn't believed he was the cause of JFK's ultimate drug-induced psychosis? Had JFK not been suffering the side effects of drugs that threatened his mental stability, there might have been no need to assassinate him.

Had Kennedy stabilized after the Vienna Summit and the Cuban missile crisis, worries about his psychological condition might have abated. Had JFK not been on methamphetamines, and had he not been suffering from the side effects of drugs that threatened his mental stability, perhaps there would have been no assassination plot. But he only got worse. And his psychotic breakdown at the Carlyle Hotel was an example of what Jacobson's drugs could do and was a portent of worse things to come. What if word leaked out about the president's instability? What kind of leverage would that give the KGB? There was too much at stake, and the CIA had to make its point: Don't cross us.

Now even LBJ knew about JFK's life-threatening conditions and his reliance on drugs. He was told about it by Richard Nixon and understood what the conspirators wanted from him: in the wake of an assassination, a quick, down-and-dirty investigation to throw the blame on the anointed lone gunman and close the case down. Johnson agreed, and the plot was put into motion.

In most difficult homicide investigations, especially serial killer investigations, a good detective begins with no presuppositions or prejudgments, but often will look for the earliest witnesses to get first impressions of what people saw. Beginning with that premise, one should ask what the most credible eyewitness saw, one of the individuals closest to the crime. That would be retired Secret Service Special Agent Paul Landis, assigned to the First Lady's detail. He guarded Jackie and the children. In his interview with the authors and in his statement to the Warren Commission, he gave a minute-by-minute account of the events of November 22, 1963, from the arrival of the First Family at Love Field in Dallas to the shots that rang out across Dealy Plaza.

Special Agent Landis described how the presidential motorcade wound its way toward Dealy Plaza and passed by the Texas Book Depository as the crowds gathered to get a glimpse of the president. That's when the first shot, sounding like a crack in the distance over Landis's right shoulder, reverberated as if in an echo chamber. Landis knew immediately what it was, but did not see the president react. Maybe it had been a firecracker. At least that's what other members of the Secret Service detail seemed to think. Then there was a second shot.

Landis said, "My reaction at this time was that the shot came from somewhere towards the front, but I did not see anyone on the overpass, and looked along the right-hand side of the road." Then he saw a man running across "a grassy section towards some concrete steps and what appeared to be a low stone wall." And this is how the theory of the "grassy knoll" came into being.[45]

This is the key point of Paul Landis's observation. If the subsequent gunshots at the president came from the front of the motorcade, then there was a second shooter, and possibly a third shooter. If there were other shooters, it was a conspiracy of like-minded felons. And if there was a conspiracy, the crime could not be brushed away as the deranged act of a lone gunman. If there was no lone gunman, the investigation could not stop at Lee Harvey Oswald. But it only took a day after President Johnson returned from Dallas for his FBI director, J. Edgar Hoover, to point that out during a conversation in the Oval Office.

When, in 1997, Ladybird Johnson, the former first lady, released the tapes her husband had recorded in the Oval Office, LBJ's machinations during the assemblage of the investigative commission came to light. First, of course, was the conversation between him and J. Edgar Hoover, during which Hoover advised LBJ that his investigation revealed there was more than one Lee Harvey Oswald. In fact, records from the United States Passport Office reveal that another Lee Harvey Oswald, not matching the person shot and killed by Jack Ruby, was surveilled by the CIA during a visit to the Soviet embassy in Mexico. LBJ acknowledged Hoover's statement and on the tape advises that he and Hoover not bring it up to Allen Dulles or to the CIA. Under Texas law, controlling law at the time of the assassination, this was a conspiracy entered into by the president of the United States and the nation's chief federal law enforcement officer to obstruct justice by concealing facts. They were accessories after the fact in a capital murder case.

The LBJ tapes were even more revealing. In recorded conversations with chief justice Earl Warren of the United States Supreme Court, President Johnson said that what was most important after the assassination was to find Lee Harvey Oswald guilty as the lone gunman, entertain conspiracy theories, especially those that might point to the USSR, and close the case down. Kennedy was dead, and turning over rocks wouldn't bring him back. LBJ pushed Earl Warren until he agreed to chair the commission. And thus the cover-up operation was set into motion.

There were, of course, records from the Parkland Hospital emergency room that revealed the location of Kennedy's gunshot wounds. The Warren Commission solution was not to examine the Parkland Hospital records directly. Instead, the Commission relied on the records of the autopsy from Bethesda Naval Hospital, where Kennedy's body was taken after Parkland. In other words, whatever the records from the immediate examination of the president's wounds at Parkland, those records were ignored in favor of a second examination at Bethesda, an examination that would actually alter the medical records. Researchers have argued that there are questions regarding the nature of JFK's gunshot wounds, as noted by doctors at Parkland, compared to the wounds noted by doctors at the Bethesda autopsy, the only records that the Warren Commission examined.

Once the president was brought to Parkland still breathing, the doctor performed a tracheotomy to establish an airway through the gunshot wound in JFK's throat. The bullet entry wound was still recognizable after the tracheotomy, however. Nevertheless Admiral Burkley, the same doctor who wanted Jacobson removed from any connection to the president, did not make note of that wound nor the tracheotomy performed at Parkland. This was a major inconsistency, because a gunshot wound from the opposite direction of the Book Depository establishes another shooter, and the tracheotomy establishes that doctors at Parkland noticed that wound. Doctors at Bethesda noticed the throat wound, because they actually contacted Parkland to confirm that a tracheotomy had been performed.

But it gets worse.

Doctors at Parkland, as well as the Catholic priest who performed the last rites over the president's body, noticed what they referred to as an "entrance wound" above the president's left front temple. An entrance wound means that a bullet had entered from the front of the motorcade, which is what Secret Service Special Agent Paul Landis believed he perceived. There was a news briefing at Parkland in which that head entrance wound was described, but the Secret Service never provided records of that briefing to the Warren Commission. In fact, the Warren Commission, supposedly a homicide investigation, did not receive the JFK medical exam records from Parkland, which in the real world of homicide investigations would be an absolutely mandatory set of data. An oversight? We think not.

Mysteriously, the entrance wound to Kennedy's skull—referred to by Parkland doctors, the priest, and which was the subject of a news briefing—simply disappeared by the time Kennedy's body got to Bethesda, because the Bethesda autopsy records don't mention it. Accordingly, we have the Secret Service not providing data about that wound to the Warren Commission—which it was required to do as a matter of law and police procedure—and the medical examiners at Bethesda not mentioning any skull entrance wound from the front. Did it simply disappear all by itself, or was there something else at work?

If there was an entrance wound to the front of the president's skull, there should have been an exit wound somewhere toward the rear of the skull if the wound was a "through and through." In fact, there was just such a wound. The explosion from the exit wound was witnessed by Secret Service Special Agent Paul Landis, who said that he saw the president's head explode in the limo when he heard the shot from the front. That exit wound was discovered and recorded at Parkland, where doctors made a sketch of the wound, and FBI agents at the autopsy procedure mentioned in their report that so much of the president's head was blown away by the exiting bullet that the brain could have been lifted right out of the skull. But this information was never publicly reviewed by the Warren Commission.

Then there is the strange back wound that the Warren Commission noted, a back entrance wound that seemed to align with the throat wound. However, there were no metallic fragments from a bullet in the wound, even though the wound was not a "through and through," but only penetrated part of the way. Worse, none of the doctors at Parkland had noticed that wound. Even worse, the Bethesda autopsy report moved the wound from lower in the back to higher near the nape of the neck, about four inches, so that it would coincide with the throat wound. Evidence, in this one instance, was not only omitted, but altered to fit the lone gunman scenario. Why would they do this even before the Warren Commission was empaneled?

An answer may lie in Lyndon Johnson's own words. In a phone conversation with Warren Commission member Senator Richard Russell, a conversation that was recorded on the LBJ Oval Office tapes and released by Ladybird Johnson, the president tells Senator Russell, a deep and antagonistic skeptic regarding the magic bullet theory (the theory suggesting that a single bullet could stop in mid-air after passing through the president, make a U-turn, and hit Texas Governor John Connolly), that LBJ, too, has no faith in the single bullet theory. That theory, by the way, was promulgated by a Warren Commission investigator, the late Republican-then-Democratic senator from Pennsylvania, Arlen Specter. Senator Russell argued that the theory made no sense and that neither he nor his Warren Commission colleague representative, later president, Gerald Ford would buy into it. But President Johnson, ultimately and logically persuasive, argued that with no single bullet theory, there could be no lone gunman. With no lone gunman, there would be a conspiracy. With a conspiracy, the case would linger until, heaven forbid, the finger of suspicion would point to the Soviets. If the Soviets were thought to be responsible for the death of President Kennedy, the United States would clamor for war, a war in which scores of millions of civilians in both countries would die. And die for what? For someone who was dead and would never come back? Was the death of one person a causa belli for the deaths of scores of millions? Senator Russell had to agree, and he also agreed to bring Representative Ford—later himself the target of two assassination attempts by members of the Charles Manson Gang—along. And that was how the Warren Commission closed its case against Oswald, who had already been murdered by Jack Ruby, heavily in debt to the Chicago mob headed by Sam Giancana.

A footnote to the Kennedy assassination is the October 12, 1964, murder of Washington, D.C., socialite and JFK mistress Mary Pinchot Meyer, who was also the former wife of CIA agent Cord Meyer. According to Peter Janney, author of *Mary's Mosaic*,[46] the CIA was behind Meyer's murder, just as it had been behind the death of President Kennedy, according to a statement by Cord Meyer. When author C. David Heyman asked Cord Meyer who had killed Mary, he replied, "The same sons of bitches that killed John F. Kennedy."[47]

How does any of this involve Max Jacobson?

Mary Meyer had been one of Jacobson's patients. She also was sexually intimate with JFK. When the CIA realized that Kennedy had revealed state secrets to Marilyn Monroe, they assumed he was also talking to the very socially connected Mary Meyer. They also knew through family friend James Jesus Angelton that Meyer kept a diary. Had she recorded classified information in it? According to

Tony Bradlee, Mary's sister and the former wife of the *Washington Post*'s Ben Bradlee, Meyer's diary contained information that JFK had divulged to her while under the influence of LSD. Meyer was friendly with Timothy Leary, as was Max Jacobson, and provided LSD to Jack Kennedy. There was no way for the CIA to find out what Meyer knew without interrogating her, which they were reluctant to do because of her Washington connections. There was only one alternative: to have her killed. Almost a year after Kennedy's assassination, Meyer was murdered along a secluded path by a canal in Georgetown. Her brother-in-law, Ben Bradlee, noticed that her house had been broken into and discovered none other than CIA counterespionage chief James Jesus Angelton looking through Mary's desk. Because Angelton was a friend, Bradlee gave him Meyer's diary, which Angelton returned without comment, presumably either having found what he was looking for or assuring himself that no secrets had turned up in it. With Mary out of the way, any secrets that a drug-addled Jack Kennedy had told her had gone to their respective graves.

As tangential as Max Jacobson's relationship was to these historic events, it can be argued that Kennedy's presidency might have taken a very different course had he not been suffering from psychotic breaks that resulted from his drug dependency. In the eyes of the CIA, Jacobson's injections had put the office of the presidency, the nation, and perhaps the entire civilized world, at risk. Had it not been for Max Jacobson and his influence on the president of the United States, history might have taken an entirely different course.

Chapter 11

The Whistle Blower

One of the most revealing sources about the medical practices of Dr. Max Jacobson was his employee and part-time actor Harvey Mann. Mann primarily worked for Jacobson as an office assistant, answering calls, making appointments, and sweeping floors. According to Jacobson's friend Alvin Aronson, Mann approached playwright Alan Jay Lerner with a threat to expose Max. Lerner knew Mann was extorting him. "Lerner, whom I was working for at that time, promised to get him work in Los Angeles. . . . When the jobs didn't pan out, Mann followed through on his threats and reported [Max]," claimed Aronson.[48] Mann reported Jacobson to the *New York Times* at about the same time that reporters for the *Times* were investigating a story about vice president Spiro Agnew's receiving methamphetamine injections from Jacobson.

When the *New York Times* published its exposé of Jacobson on December 4, 1972, it made no mention of Harvey Mann, even though he claimed to author A. E. Hotchner that he had been the one to tip off the *Times*. In his book, *Choice People: The Greats, Near-*

Greats, and Ingrates I Have Known, Hotchner reveals what Mann told him about Max Jacobson. Hotchner's literary agent, Audrey Wood, had told him about "a young man, sent by a doctor friend of mine, who has a compelling story that I'd like you to hear. I think it's something you may want to write about."[49] She then told him that it concerned Max Jacobson, who was being exposed by the *New York Times*. Wood said that "Mann is ready to tell everything, his own story, which, believe me, is frightening and terrible, as well as what he knows about all the people whom Jacobson treated while Mann worked for him—from President Kennedy to Truman Capote." [50] After watching the death of a friend from amphetamines, Hotchner thought that telling Mann's story might be "an effective way to expose speed and the Mephistophelian speed doctors, who quietly and legally speed up the lives of their patients, faster and faster 'til many of them spin out of control. . . . Harvey Mann might be a way to tell the story as it should be told—from the inside out."[51] Mann agreed to meet with Hotchner to tell his story.

When director Yul Brynner sent fourteen-year-old Mann to see Jacobson for a bad cold, Mann was immediately struck by Jacobson's appearance. According to Mann, Jacobson was "a powerful man, enormous trunk, huge steely arms. . . . The way he looked at me, his voice, the whole thing, I just felt I was in the presence of God."[52] He said Jacobson never examined him, nor did he ever see Jacobson examine a patient in all the years he worked for him. He gave him three injections while informing him that he would make him "look like an actor," and Mann felt reenergized. After that, he became a frequent patient and started hanging around Jacobson's office. By the time he was in his early twenties, he was working for the doctor full time. Jacobson soon had Mann injecting patients—"me, with absolutely no training, of any kind"[53]—and preparing the mixtures. "I helped prepare some of his new, experimental stuff, like the extract from the glands of an electric eel, and an extract made from the bone marrow of beef. He tried them on me—the marrow shot caused me to break out in sores like cigarette burns all over my body; the eel injection hurt painfully for more than a year, caused me to run a high temperature, and left me feeling numb in my hip."[54] He told Hotchner, "Max thought he could cure anything with shots. Once, after giving me shots, he tore off my glasses and broke them and told me I could see now; my eyesight was cured. Of course that was ridiculous—without glasses I was Helen Keller."[55]

Jacobson also created a package of skin cream in his lab, Mann said, that he sold to cure all kinds of skin conditions from acne to cancer. "It was made up of Nivea cream, vitamins, and all the leftovers of what was injected into patients the last week, including hormones and what not. . . . He sold an enormous number of those jars at forty dollars each. . . . We called it Max's chicken fat."[56] Mann showed Hotchner proof of his employment with Jacobson, including tax forms. He told Hotchner, in great detail, about his treatment of famous patients, including legendary pianist Harvey Lavan "Van" Cliburn. He recounted to Hotchner, "Van made it big with his Russian performance, and he was hooked on Max's injections. . . . When Van returned back to New York for his Carnegie recital, he developed an infection in a cuticle on one of his fingers that Max treated. . . . Max injected the infection with collagen . . . however, his finger swelled up as thick as his wrist. . . . Van's manager rushed him to the Hospital for Joint Diseases, where an emergency team of surgeons went to work on his finger. Later on, Van told me that the head surgeon had said that another hour or so they might have been forced to amputate the finger . . . but a week later Van was back in Max's office getting his regular shot."[57]

Mann told Hotchner that Jacobson treated many of his patients free of charge. "Max had a lot of creative people he carried during lean times. Max didn't really care all that [much] about money. What really mattered to Max was that all these people were dependent on him. . . . In his office, Max was King."[58] Harvey recalled to Hotchner that "almost any hour of the day or night, if you wanted a shot, Max was there to give it to you. I sometimes came to Max's waiting room at two, three in the morning, and there'd be twenty people sitting around, waiting their turn. You see, speed people can't sleep. They're high all the time. . . . Some people like Marlene Dietrich just maintained a level and to hell with sleep. . . ."[59]

Mann confirmed that Jacobson had given Kennedy injections while at the Vienna Summit. "I can prove it," he said.[60]

Mann also had an interesting perspective on the way Jacobson's drug cocktails interacted with his patients: "The injection itself gives you the initial flash; the needle actually feels red-hot going in, and you get a reaction in your testicles just like an orgasm, your testicles feel hot as hell, your feet rise above the ground, you feel like you're in heat, like you could have multiple orgasms. It's the calcium-niacin combination [that] gives you that, and it's no wonder those injections hooked all of us."[61]

Mann presented Hotchner with three shopping bags full of material that included an A to Z file of Jacobson's celebrity patients. This index contained cards for, among others, Otto Preminger, Lee Radziwill, Andy Williams, Eartha Kitt, Hermione Gingold, Pablo Casals, Gertrude Lawrence, Sheilah Graham, Margaret Leighton, Katherine Dunham, Montgomery Clift, Hedy Lamarr, Maurice Chevalier, and Zero Mostel. He told Hotchner about loading Jacobson's medical bag himself when he was summoned to the Carlyle

Hotel by the president. One of the most shocking stories Mann revealed to Hotchner was how Jacobson poisoned his wife, Nina, with his magic elixir:

> I spent a lot of time in Max's apartment. I was virtually one of the family. I got to know Nina very well. . . . She became addicted to the amphetamine mix that Max was feeding her. Nina was a woman of Garboesque beauty. . . . She was an artist, a truly lovely woman, well bred, intelligent, and the slow tragic death which I observed her suffer had a profound effect on me. At the time she died she was thin as my finger, wasted away, a terrible tragedy.[62]

Mann told Hotchner of Jacobson's use of amphetamines on himself: "Max is hard pressed to find a vein in his body he can get a needle into. They're all collapsed. Shot out. . . . Max literally injects himself every couple of hours. . . . It's been going on for thirty years. . . . He never sleeps."[63] Mann said that Max's injections had nearly driven him to suicide:

> After all those years of accelerated injections, I really began to come apart. . . . I attempted suicide but I was saved by my sister. . . . I was in a deep amphetamine coma, and when they got me to Lenox Hill Hospital, I was declared dead on arrival. . . . The doctors finally diagnosed it as amphetamine poisoning. . . . The first thing I did when I got out of the hospital was to go to Max for a shot. . . . After another year, I was more hooked than ever. . . . In another couple of months, I'm sure I would have been as dead as Mark Shaw and Nina and some of the others I haven't told you about.[64]

With the help of a friend, Mann entered Alcoholics Anonymous, but told Hotchner, "I'm still unused to a life without the crutch of Max's injections. After all, that's all the life I had for more than twenty years."[65]

While talking to Hotchner during Jacobson's state license revocation hearings, Mann had been asked by the doctor in charge of the investigation to wait before publicly exposing Jacobson until the hearings were complete. The hearings took fourteen months before a five-doctor panel. Jacobson's attorney, Simon Rose of the Louis Nizer firm, had prepared one of the best defenses the board had ever encountered. There were four thousand pages of testimony, more than ninety witnesses (most of whom were current or former patients), and countless pieces of evidence and exhibits. The New York state medical board ultimately revoked Jacobson's license to practice medicine.

Hotchner concluded that although Harvey Mann suffered heinously from Jacobson's drugs, "he had the ultimate satisfaction of knowing that by triggering this investigation, he had deterred others from being as victimized as he had been."[66]

Chapter 12

The Final Days

As the 1960s came to a close, Max was facing serious questions about his practice and methods on several fronts. First, the federal Bureau of Narcotics and Dangerous Drugs (BNDD) had been investigating Max for about five years prior to the 1972 *New York Times* exposé of Max's practices. A review by the BNDD showed that a substantial amount of the amphetamines he had purchased were unaccounted for. Where had they gone? Were there undisclosed purchases of Max's drugs?

The BNDD had raided Max's office in 1969, where they found conditions beyond unsanitary, and he was facing disciplinary charges as a result of that search. Second, several of Jacobson's patients had reported him to authorizing agencies regarding his so-called "vitamin" injections. Film director Otto Preminger, who had a severe reaction to several of the doctor's injections, reported him to the AMA.

Actor and Max's former lab assistant Felice Orlandi, after a severe nervous breakdown that resulted in a prolonged hospitalization due to an overdose of methamphetamine injections, reported Max to the New York Medical Society. And the key complaint to both the *New York Times* and the State Board of Regents in 1969, made by Mark Shaw's ex-wife, Gerri Trotta, was that Jacobson murdered his friend Shaw by methamphetamine poisoning. Although there was some investigation from Trotta's claims, they never resulted in any criminal charges, formal or informal. Until the Controlled Substances Act was enacted in 1970, there were no real regulations regarding the use and dispensation of amphetamines. By 1970, however, amphetamine use by civilians became illegal with the passage of the U.S. Drug Abuse Regulation and Control Act. As a result, official government regulatory agencies began controlling distribution of the drug.

The investigations into the distribution of methamphetamines circled around Max Jacobson's medical practice. But Jacobson believed that his methamphetamine injections could help heroin addicts free themselves from the drug. Unfortunately, that freedom came at the expense of addiction to meth. However, Jacobson was unafraid to make his opinions known. Thus, at the invitation of his friend and patient, representative Claude Pepper from Florida, Jacobson appeared before the House Select Committee on Crime on June 30, 1970, to discuss the treatment of heroin addiction. The biography Jacobson submitted to the committee contained this passage:

Dr. Jacobson is particularly interested in using his methods to counteract the severe physical and emotional stresses of those who live and work in environments of continual high pressure. . . . In this context he has been entrusted with the supervision of the health of a large number of highly-placed government officials, including several heads of state, numerous business and industrial leaders, and a great many top-rank members of the performing arts.[67]

Representative Pepper concurred, stating at the hearing, "I have known Dr. Jacobson for a long time and have the highest esteem for his professional excellence and for his achievements. He treated some of the most important and distinguished patients in the world, and I think he is a man of extraordinary professional skill and is particularly imaginative."[68] This testimony all occurred after the raid by the BNDD the year before, which became part of the investigation into Max's practices that had been ongoing for nearly five years.

Despite Jacobson's protestations of his good faith in treating patients, questions still arose about the levels of methamphetamine he was manufacturing, where the ingredients for his concoctions came from, and how the drugs were distributed. Max argued that he was simply supplying his MS patients with his injections to keep them free of pain and fatigue, running his research into the disease through his nonprofit corporation, the Constructive Research Foundation, on Long Island. Max had even hired the advertising agency McCann Erickson in 1969 to market his self-described research operation, the Constructive Research Foundation. That corporation still exists today, more than twenty-five years after Jacobson's death.

One of the many events triggering close scrutiny of Jacobson's medical practices and, ultimately, the *New York Times* exposé of him was the death of patient Mark Shaw. Had Max murdered him by overdosing him on his drugs? Dr. Michael M. Baden, the associate medical examiner of New York City, who performed the autopsy on Mark Shaw, agreed with Secret Service Agent and Shaw's

149

close friend Paul Landis regarding overdoses of methamphetamine. Landis said he believed that Shaw had been overdosed to the point of death. He pointed to the fact that Mark Shaw was only forty-seven when he died in his Kips Bay apartment in Manhattan on January 26, 1969. According to *New York Times* reporter Boyce Rensberger, when the medical examiner's office called Jacobson, he insisted that Shaw had a history of heart disease and that he had died of a heart attack. The autopsy showed another cause. There was no evidence of heart disease, but Mr. Shaw's internal organs were laden with methamphetamine residue. There was heavy scarring and discoloration along the veins in his arms—the tracks of someone who repeatedly injects himself with drugs. The death was ruled by the New York medical examiner as "acute and chronic intravenous amphetamine poisoning." Yet there were no charges brought against Dr. Jacobson. According to Michael Samek, Jacobson was friends with New York attorney general Louis K. Lefkowitz, who, according to Samek, had the issue swept under the rug and kept out of the publications.

Despite all the loud complaints regarding Jacobson that were breaking the surface tension of public knowledge, the *New York Times*, where rumors about Max and his celebrity clientele were circulating, did not know about the dispensation of drugs at Max's all-night parties at his office. Nor did the staff know that right across town from the *Times* offices, there was a doctor who was treating and thus controlling some of the most important icons of the twentieth century. But the *Times* would soon begin its own investigation as the forces in the media, smelling blood on the water, began to circle around the presidency of Richard Nixon and the rumors about Nixon's possible connection to this strange Dr. Feelgood, who was distributing an energy-boosting magic elixir.

In late September 1972, a high-ranking, credible source gave a tip to an editor at the *New York Times* that vice president Spiro T. Agnew was a patient of the notorious Dr. Feelgood. When this report came to the editor, the *Times,* considered by its influential readers to be at the cutting edge of all media, had just been eclipsed by the *Washington Post*'s coverage of the unfolding Watergate story. Some media historians have said that the *Times* held back while the *Post* forged ahead. If the publishing executives at the *Times* believed that their investigative reporters had been relegated to back-draft of an exposé of Nixon and Watergate, the Dr. Feelgood story with the Agnew connection was tantalizing. Perhaps against the background of the unfolding Watergate story, two of the *Times*'s leading health journalists were assigned to find out about Dr. Max. There was the scent of a scandal in the air, perhaps a greater conspiracy, and Boyce Rensberger and Lawrence K. Altman, M.D., were on the case.

Boyce Rensberger was a science writer at the *Times.* He had joined the *Times* in 1971 after a stint as a science editor at the *Detroit Free Press.* Dr. Lawrence Altman became the *New York Times*'s medical correspondent in 1969. The authors interviewed both Mr. Rensberger and Dr. Altman, along with noted *Times* health journalist Jane Brody, on their perspectives of Dr. Jacobson and the pieces that appeared in the *Times* about Max.

Rensberger recalled first staking out, from his car, the 87th Street offices of Jacobson with Altman. They noticed several noted personalities leaving the building. In fact, what they noticed was an ongoing stream of people they recognized—celebrities, literary figures, and the like—entering the building. What was going on in there, and why had Vice President Agnew's name come up?

The burning questions were who was Dr. Feelgood, and what

was going on in this office? For almost twenty years, Dr. Max had flown under the *Times's* radar. Yes, stories about which celebrities were on drugs had surfaced and then disappeared. Rumors abounded about the strange man with the accent whom reporters had seen around President Kennedy. But the stories went nowhere because Kennedy's real physiological problems were hidden from the public, with press complicity, much like Woodrow Wilson's incapacitating stroke and FDR's paralysis were kept hidden from the public. But this was a different era. Watergate was breaking. The Pentagon Papers story was brewing. Nixon was facing a circle of critics who were closing in. Rules had changed, journalistic gladiatorial combat was in the offing, and the gloves had come off.

The *Times* reporters smelled a real scandal with potentially wide-reaching repercussions. Here was a physician who had been out front as drugging world leaders, iconic actors, singers, opera stars, writers, director, producers, and the cream of the New York literati. And then there were the stories about Jacobson and JFK and the influence Jacobson exerted with his drugs, especially at the disastrous Vienna Summit, the results of which had been reported a decade earlier by *Times* reporter James Reston.

The late-night parties at Max's office, the names of movie stars, writers, politicians, and celebrities who attended the parties, and the dispensation of drugs were all taking place in the *Times's* own home city. Yet none of this had been made public. But all of that was about to change.

Times reporters Rensberger and Altman were handed the assignment to find out if the rumor about Agnew seeking amphetamines was true. They went to Jacobson's office to talk to the doctor, but Jacobson did not view the reporters as investigators. He truly believed, according to Mike Samek, that he was now going to receive his day in the sun. He was going to be recognized for his work and get the acceptance he had sought. For a sociopathic narcissist, it was a dream come true. Jacobson was never shy about boasting about his famous patients. According to Rensberger, he once boasted about how many celebrities' careers he had made possible. He told composer Burton Lane's wife during a preview of Lerner's *On a Clear Day You Can See Forever*, that he had worked with the Kennedys and showed her his tie clip, which had a PT-109 insignia. Max boasted further that he had traveled with the Kennedys and treated Jack and Jackie Kennedy, who, he said, could not have made it without him. And he boasted that Kennedy have him the tie clip in gratitude.

Now, talking to Rensberger and Altman, Max imagined he would become the long-awaited and acknowledged medical miracle man, the savior of presidents, statesmen, and artists. He could come out of his lab and be touted to the world. Jacobson went full-out to impress the reporters. He now had his platform for glory.

Jacobson took Rensberger and Altman on a grand tour of his medical practice. Altman, in an interview with the authors, recalled that at some point in the interview with Jacobson, Max excused himself to go to the restroom. Rensberger recalled that "when he returned from the bathroom, I noticed blood droplets on his arm; he had just shot-up. . . . Max bragged about his laboratory, which was located in the office. . . . It was filthy, there was garbage on the floor. . . . He was dressed in rumpled clothes, a stained lab-coat. . . . He had dirty fingernails. . . . He had a deep accent but it was less than Kissinger. . . . He looked younger than seventy-two."[69]

Both Altman and Rensberger recalled Jacobson's showing him a vial of his drug with "rocks" at the bottom that he said were "radio-active" and gave the patient "extra energy." He would not tell Alt-

153

man the contents of the vial. Rensberger commented that Jacobson did not strike him as "intelligent" but "acted compassionate, had a great bedside manner when we watched him with a patient. . . . I think Max felt he was helping people . . . but most of all he had an infatuation with celebrity."[70] Jacobson told them of his safari with Prince Radziwill, explained how he was Cecil B. DeMille's personal physician in Egypt during the filming of *The Ten Commandments*, and showed them Eddie Fisher's picture at Max's wedding to his third wife, Ruth, a photo that had Fisher's inscription, "He's still my God." Max told them of his other celebrity patients he treated, and of course he told him of how he was important to President Kennedy.

This initial meeting set off an extensive investigation of Jacobson that took nearly two months. "It took quite a while,"[71] recalled Rensberger, who headed a team with Dr. Lawrence Altman and nine other reporters, including Jane Brody, and a researcher. This team of twelve interviewed and probed Dr. Jacobson's patients, studied his records, and dissected everything there was to know about him. This became the *New York Times*'s version of a Watergate-type scandal, and the reporters had an axe to grind, perhaps wanting to prove to the world that they were still on top of what it takes to be investigative journalists. The *Times* team persevered after their first article, even in the face of the pressure they received from Jacobson's celebrity friends and patients to leave him alone. The reporters would not yield to that pressure.

Jacobson, still deluding himself about the public admiration that would be coming his way, was totally unaware that this was going to be an investigation into his practices, an investigation that could trigger a professional investigation that would bring about the demise of his medical career. He asked his friends and famous patients to cooperate with the reporters. He believed that this was going to be his "coming-out party," and in that he was not far from the truth. But it was a truth he never suspected when the *Times* outed him to the world.

On December 4, 1972, the Max Jacobson story splashed across the *Times* front page with the headline, "Amphetamines Used by a Physician to Lift Moods of Famous Patients."[72] Dr. Jacobson's photo was part of the front page of this multi-page story that exploded on the scene in New York and then spread like wildfire throughout the country. If Max believed he would now be even more famous, he was right. But it was infamy rather than fame.

Up until that time, each state's private medical societies, the professional associations supposedly governing practice standards, were looked on to police their own physicians. The states licensed doctors, and New York was no exception, but any malpractice or licensing deadlines were basically left to the medical societies. Accordingly, the licensing for a doctor in New York State was left up to the New York State Board of Education. Any discipline would come from a hearing before the New York State Board of Regents.

The medical societies were blamed to have done next to nothing to police their ranks. They had no legal power per se other than to deny membership, but they insisted they had an obligation to investigate complaints and turn violations over to their respective state boards. And although Jacobson's unorthodox treatments, administered under the cover of prescriptive medicine, were known to the New York County Medical Society, said radio talk show host Don Imus on his program,[73] the society neither took action against the physician nor informed the state department of education, which licenses doctors in New York. To this day, the society contends that it never received a patient complaint about Dr. Jacobson, although there remains some dispute about that claim. Members who knew, the *Times* charged in its exposé, did not inform the state because "unorthodox" medical practice is not cause to lodge a formal complaint against a colleague. There is some potential, argued the critics, for local and state societies' medical care foundations and peer review systems to not police the incompetent or negligent physician, because they were more concerned with cost and utilization control than quality control. But crusading young reporter, and current Fox television host, Geraldo Rivera also joined the chorus of those demanding that the medical board expose the practices of those doctors dispensing methamphetamines to their patients.

With news organizations revealing the secrets of Jacobson's medical practices and the New York State Department of Education conducting its hearings into Jacobson, the scandal around him grew.

Max, through Jackie Kennedy, hired the famed attorney Louis Nizer, also a patient of Jacobson. Although Nizer promised to oversee the case, it was turned over to a British associate of Nizer's firm, who was in far over his head. Max Jacobson in his unpublished memoir recalled that Chuck Spalding called him on May 28, 1973, asking to meet Max. Max's wife, who took the call, said she wanted Max to rest that day because his first medical panel hearing was on the 30th. Unless this was an "absolute necessity," she told Chuck, could they push the meeting back to the next week? This was truly important, Chuck said, and he would meet Max the next afternoon.

Chuck called Max at noon the next day and asked that he drop over to his apartment. At the door, Chuck told Max, "Here is somebody who wants to see you." Suddenly Max found himself hugging

Jackie Kennedy, who kissed him, ushered him into the room, and said she was truly upset at all the negative publicity Max was getting. Chuck politely left the room, leaving Max and Jackie together. Jackie said the whole thing was simply unfair and that Max was being targeted by the press. Jack Kennedy's reputation was also being attacked, and Max asked Jackie who was behind it. The attack on the late president was "vicious," Max said, reminding her of all that he did for the president. It was Max's doing that kept the president functioning on the trip to Vienna and to Paris and London. Kennedy performed even though he was under crushing pressures from the import of the summit meetings. But Max had been there, he said, whenever Kennedy needed him, at the United Nations, Carlyle, Washington, Hyannis Port, Gelnars, and West Palm Beach. And Max never asked for a fee.

Chuck Spalding might have called for the meeting, but it was Jackie who was behind it. She was the one who had wanted to meet, wanting to know what Max would say if someone on the panel brought up the stories of Max at the White House. There would be no problem, Max told her, because his regard for medical ethics and discretion when it came to discussing his patients had been part of him for fifty years of practice. He would not broach confidentiality now. Besides, he said, his conscience was completely clear. He had nothing to hide because he was doing the best for his patients.

Max told Jackie Kennedy, whom he had treated a decade earlier, that he was worried about the panel's license review hearings, explaining that he had already spent $35,000 in legal fees, and this was even before the hearings commenced. He was, he continued, owed $12,000 from his Constructive Research Foundation, money he was due but never collected, mainly because, he claimed, he was never concerned about money, especially from the president. But he was running a huge legal bill and had to be reimbursed.

"Don't worry," Jackie reportedly told him. "All will be taken care of." It wasn't.

After the meeting, as Spalding escorted Max downstairs, he assured him that help was on the way, suggesting that the foundation write to Jackie addressed to his attention, requesting a contribution, which could then be paid to Max through the foundation instead of through the Kennedys. As relieved as Max said he was after the two-hour conversation with Jackie, the help that Jackie and Spalding promised him never came through. Max was on his own, even though he had promised Jackie Kennedy and Chuck Spalding that he would keep the secret about his treatments of President Kennedy. Max reportedly told them that doctors always keep their patients' records confidential. But the British newspapers had picked up the story of the Jacobson scandal from the *New York Times* and from Geraldo Rivera's reporting on New York's Channel 7, and they spread the news about rumors concerning Jacobson's treatment of the late President Kennedy.

Another ironic twist to the Jacobson/Kennedy connection that was later reported was that Jacobson's shots have been speculated as one of the causes of Jackie's lymphoma that she suffered many years later. C. David Heymann revealed in his book *American Legacy: The Story of John and Caroline Kennedy*, with John F. Kennedy, Jr., that shortly before his death, John Kennedy, Jr., said that he fully believed that Jacobson's injections brought on his mother's lymphoma. He based this on a study by the American Multicenter Cohort (MACS) of nearly 2,500 patients, which showed that those who used amphetamines frequently, in the amount of once weekly or more, were nearly five times more likely to develop lymphoma than patients who did not use amphetamines as often.

Max's first hearing before his license revocation hearing began on May 30, 1973. The charges against Max stated that the New York state investigation resulted in forty-eight counts of unprofessional conduct and fraud in the practice of medicine. At the later hearings in April 1974, the state medical board accused the doctor of giving himself depressant and stimulant drugs for nonmedical purposes, failing to oversee use of such drugs by his patients and employees, failing to adequately examine patients prior to giving them depressants or stimulants, and manufacturing, selling, and delivering adulterated and misbranded drugs not adequately tested for safety, strength, identity, quality, or purity. There were also charges for failure to obtain required applications to test and administer new drugs, failure to keep accurate records of controlled drugs, and selling drugs without the required professional order from the purchaser.

It was former employee Harvey Mann who finally blew the whistle on Max. He gave a firsthand account of the laboratories, the inner workings of the office, how Mann as an out-of-work actor was giving intravenous shots in Max's office until he nearly killed someone with an air pocket, and how he manufactured drugs that Jacobson shipped as product worldwide. Mann had been a patient of Max since he was fourteen and began to work for him when he was twenty. Others testifying against Max included his nurse Ruth Mosse, actor and former employee Felice Orlando, Otto Preminger, Gerri Trotta (who was Mark Shaw's first wife), and several former patients who were not identified. One of the patient's testimonies was, "My last shot was a blood-red thing about a foot long. I went blind for two days, and when my eyesight finally came back, I threw away all my speed and hung up my works on the living room lamp-shade."

It was revealed in the report and hearing that the investigators found evidence that at least 90 percent of the doctor's patients were self-injecting his mixtures. The heavy volume of injections was reflected by the fact that for the periods 1964 to1966 and 1968 to 1972, Jacobson's office used 463,719 hypodermic needles and 236,646 syringes. This averages out to 1,920 needles and syringes per week, indicating that multiple patients were self-injecting. The investigators were also concerned by the relatively relaxed steriliza-tion standards in the laboratory, including an incident that was re-ported on October 26, 1970, revealing that "placenta was observed in respondent's refrigerator dated August 1970, next to bread, sand-wiches, storage batteries, and various other types of lunch compo-nents."[74]

The New York State Board of Regents finally ruled on April 25, 1975, that the State Board of Education revoke Max Jacobson's medical license for unprofessional conduct. In a unanimous action, the doctor was found guilty on forty-eight counts of unprofessional conduct in eleven specifications and an additional count of fraud or deceit. The decision was based on a 42-page report itemizing 235 findings of fact about Jacobson's career. Among other things, the document charged he had administered amphetamines without sound medical justification, failed to keep required records on use of controlled drugs, was unable to account for quantities of drugs, and misrepresented injections as treatment for MS without medical evidence.

The *New York Times* headline the next day read, "Jacobson Loses License."[75] The story reported that the New York State Board of

Regents had pulled Max's medical license and that he would no longer be authorized to practice medicine in the state. The *Times* documented the charges against him that the Board of Regents had substantiated and revealed that many of Jacobson's celebrity clients suffered as a result of his treatments. But the story didn't stop there.

The hearings against Max set off a firestorm across the nation, resulting in a host of new laws and regulations. Where the various state medical societies had historically policed their own ranks, most states now enacted laws that set up boards of ethics, and soon they oversaw all medical doctors. No longer would the physicians be allowed to go unregulated and not under government control. On March 28, 1973, President Richard Nixon signed Reorganization Plan No. 2 of 1973 proposing the creation of the Drug Enforcement Administration (DEA). Congress accepted the proposal on July 1, 1973, officially establishing the DEA. The War on Drugs, partly inspired by the Max Jacobson case and resulting scandal, had begun.

Max felt he was the "scapegoat" of the FDA, commenting to his friends that if someone asked what amphetamine was, he would answer that amphetamine is simply a drug a doctor prescribes to stimulate the central nervous system and energize the recipient's body. In Max's era, even before the early 1960s, amphetamines were prescribed as a weight reducer, particularly for arthritis patients and cardiovascular disease, because weight reduction was a key to longevity and mitigation of pain. But doctors also prescribed amphetamines for a variety of medical problems, including hypertension, diabetes, and in preparation for surgery. Women, too, were prescribed amphetamines for obstetrics and gynecological issues. Amphetamine was prescribed for the treatment of a variety of neurological and psychiatric issues, including narcolepsy, alcoholism, mental depression, post-encephalitic Parkinsonism, barbiturate or morphine poisoning, fatigue, spasm of the gastrointestinal tract, and menstrual cramps. In short, Max believed, amphetamines were routinely prescribed, not just by him, but by other doctors, to make patients feel good by reducing the symptoms that caused them suffering.

Max contended that when amphetamine prescriptions and dosages were left in the hands of the doctor, the administration of the drug was strictly a matter of a doctor/patient relationship. This controlled the illegal purchases of the drug while also controlling the drug's distribution. However, because the newly created Food and Drug Administration needed to justify its own existence and make sure its workers were paid, the agency needed a scapegoat. That scapegoat was Max Jacobson, the poster boy for drug abuse and distribution. Max seemd to actually believe this.

Max began a series of appeals to regain his license. He closed his 87th Street office and worked out of his apartment at 305 West 86th Street. Many of his patients visited him, including author Roger Rapoport, who wrote a chapter about Max in his book *The Super-Doctors*; actor/playwright Alvin Aronson said that "we would go into one of his bedrooms" for treatment. Mike Samek said that Max was definitely changed, "but he still continued his practice at his apartment."[76] And Eddie Fisher said, "I still saw Max [at] his place,"[77] but that his glory days were definitely over. Max had to remain out of the spotlight, and his patients visited him strictly on the down-low. Everyone was aware that Max had lost his license. Miracle Max was legally barred from medical practice.

After he lost his license, Max continued to stay physically active, swimming in his apartment building's pool every day, which made him look younger than his years. But the final blow struck him when his attempt to regain his license failed, and the state Board of Regents denied his reinstatement in May 1979. A state spokesmen noted that the then seventy-nine-year-old Jacobson didn't seem ready to enter into the "mainstream of practice" again. Then, in June 1979, the prestigious Pasteur Institute in Paris, of which Max was proudly a member and where he had hospital privileges since he was a physician in Paris in the early 1930s, stripped him of his affiliation because they questioned the legitimacy of the treatments he was providing. Max had lived to be a physician. It was his life's goal. He realized on the loss of his appeal and his losing the affiliation with the Pasteur Institute that he would soon be fully branded a charlatan and would have to live life as a civilian. His powers as a medical wizard had been stripped.

"I visited Max and Ruth at their apartment around two weeks prior to Max's death. He was undoubtedly a broken man," recalled Alvin Aronson.[78]

"The end for Max was horrible," recalled Eddie Fisher. "The last time I saw Max was at his wedding in 1973; I think it was in Vegas. But it wasn't really Max; he was a shadow of what he was. . . . It was after he was being crucified in the newspapers. . . . It was what was left of a crazy genius. . . . His own drugs had destroyed him. . . . At the wedding reception his wife, Ruth, who was a nurse from his office, had to feed him. And then she took him into a private room and gave him a dose of his own medicine. . . . Although many people wanted him prosecuted, he ended up working quietly in the back room of another doctor's office for about three years. . . . When he died, he had become his last victim."[79]

After his death, there was no obituary for Max in the *New York Times*. Alvin Aronson said that he and his wife had dinner with Ruth

Jacobson a couple of weeks after his death, where she told him, "I won't give those bastards any money. I don't want his obituary in that rag."[80]

Chapter 13

Miracle Max or Mad Max?

The Jacobson story turns out to be a story of how one man dispensing powerful methamphetamines not only changed the course of US presidential history, but also wound up creating what amounted to nothing less than a subculture of celebrity addicts. As a result, Jacobson ultimately became an instrument for the media in their pursuit of Richard Nixon, even while his actions helped convince President Nixon to launch the War on Drugs.

In his book *Ailing, Aging, Addicted: Studies of Compromised Leadership*, author Dr. Bert E. Park presents an intriguing analogy relevant not only to JFK's situation, but also to Max Jacobson's. Park strongly argued that Jacobson was a sociopath, a quack, and a financial opportunist. Park draws a strong parallel between the relationship of Adolf Hitler to his private doctor, amphetamine specialist Dr. Theodore Morell, and that of John F. Kennedy to Dr. Max Jacobson. Park suggests that Morell had so thoroughly drugged Hitler to the point where he became even more psychotic, paranoid, and delusional than he already was, committing resources to an unsustainable invasion of the Soviet Union. Even Hitler's generals realized how demented their leader was and plotted his assassination. Did those behind the Kennedy assassination see a similarity between what the German generals did and what they had to do? Park also theorizes what might have occurred if JFK had not been assassinated in 1963 and had continued to be treated by Jacobson, suggesting that Kennedy might have become completely irrational; with his finger on a nuclear trigger, that irrationality could have been very dangerous. The dangers of placing a patient in just such a state of irrational behavior was also suggested in Jacobson's license revocation hearing. However, Jacobson was true to his promise to Jackie Kennedy and did not elaborate on his relationship with President Kennedy and his routine visits to the White House.

In the four thousand pages of testimony assembled over a two-year period by the New York State Board of Regents Review Committee on Discipline, the White House is mentioned only once. Jacobson had kept his promise not to implicate JFK, even though Robert Kennedy had told the FBI about his brother's treatment; the story itself had eventually leaked. Privately, however, the self-assured doctor openly spelled out in his diary his treatment of JFK and the close relationship they shared.

Methamphetamine injections were all Jacobson knew, a practice he continued to use on himself and all his patients, regardless of the disease he was treating, until the day he lost his license. If Max perceived himself to be a modern-day Dr. Frankenstein, able to conquer death by rejuvenating the dying cells in a patient's body, he also had to confront Frankenstein's monster, which he never did. It was himself.

Flagrantly manufacturing his concoctions without a license to do so in his rush to dispense them day and night, Jacobson also failed to maintain adequate quality control or sterility standards. Records indicate that Jacobson's "nightly mailings left the respondent's office at the rate of 2 to 30 vials to locations throughout the United States and the world."[81] In other words, without formal approval or oversight from an authorizing agency to manufacture, sell, and ship his elixir, Max was essentially a drug pusher. Ultimately, Max was found guilty of malfeasance. In the words of the inquiry summation: "Adulterated drugs [were found] . . . consisting of filthy, putrid, and/or decomposed substances."[82] Jacobson also failed to keep proper records of the stimulants and depressants he prescribed. No doubt he dealt in large quantities, particularly when it came to staples of his pharmacopoeia, methamphetamine HCL, and dextroamphetamine sulfate. Within a two-year period alone, the doctor was unable to account for 1,474 grams of purchased methamphetamine, another count on which he was found liable.

More alarming was Jacobson's willingness to supply his patients with injectable medication to be self-administered. These patients were addicts allowed by their doctor to inject themselves with a dangerous addictive substance. By the state board estimate, at least 90 percent of his patients were afforded this dubious luxury. President Kennedy was among them. The FBI charged with analyzing these medications in 1961 uncovered five vials that Jacobson had left behind in the White House, each revealing high concentrations of amphetamines and steroids. Robert Kennedy was so alarmed by Jacobson's increasing access to his brother that he had the FDA, via the FBI, analyze fifteen separate vials he demanded from Jacobson on the spot. Both independent reports coincide with what the state later disclosed.

Jacobson never denied that he used amphetamines liberally, on himself as well as his patients. They were not illegal, nor were their negative attributes and psychologically addictive properties common knowledge outside of the medical profession. The New York State medical licensing authority had to determine whether Jacobson's self-administration of the drugs rendered him medically and psychologically incompetent to treat patients.

How had Jacobson managed to thrive for so long without being questioned? To be sure, the era in which he practiced seemed to allow for as much blue-sky thinking as legitimate science-based medicine. Snake Oil salesmen were providing self-described cures of all kinds and so-called "New Age" practitioners promised spiritual as well as physical health. American society had its share of medical charlatans and quick-fix practitioners by the 1960s, and artists and socially connected individuals flocked to them. To accommodate and exploit those socialites who were naive enough to judge a physician's credentials by his social visibility, there was much to be said for this up-and-coming immigrant German who created the impressive façade of research while cultivating a reputation as "Dr. Feelgood" among those who passed through his doors.

The cloak of legitimacy, particularly scientific legitimacy, has often masked the crass commercialism of charlatans posing as serious doctors. Adolf Hitler's doctor, Theodore Morell, who advertised himself as a skin and venereal disease expert, actually made a small fortune in the methamphetamine-laced drugs he manufactured, labeled, and sold in his own laboratories. Like Jacobson, amphetamines were the mainstay of Morell's treatment of the Fuehrer, who, like Kennedy and other celebrities, had been introduced to his future physician through social connections. Such well-placed contacts played into the hands of two physicians cut from the same cloth, motivated as they were to build a socially prominent clientele that would eventually catapult them to the attention of their respective leaders.

Did Jacobson actually perform any legitimate medical research, as he had claimed? His scientific papers, such as one published in 1968 on tissue regeneration, did not follow the protocols or steps necessary to be considered "scientific." He had never had an article accepted by the Journal of the American Medical Association. By the time the New York State Board of Regents began its investigation, Jacobson belonged to no professional societies, did not have staff privileges at any hospital in New York, and had been deemed a fraud by the official association conducting research into MS.

New York Times reporter Boyce Rensberger determined that Jacobson had purchased at least 29.7 pounds of amphetamines in five years, enough for 100,000 doses per year. He wrote,

> The doctor's office reported that Dr. Jacobson buys amphetamines at the rate of 80 grams per month. This is enough to make 100 fairly strong doses of 25 milligrams per day. According to the Federal Bureau of Narcotics and Dangerous Drugs, which investigated Jacobson at different times over almost five years, a review by the agency of the doctor's records showed a substantial quantity of the amphetamines he had purchased was unaccounted for. In 1965, the bureau ordered seizure on all controlled drugs in Dr. Jacobson's possession, an action he contested in a suit that is still pending.[83]

There were other "amphetamine" physicians who had started up practices in Manhattan, namely Dr. Robert Freymann and Dr. John Bishop. Freymann, like Jacobson, had escaped Nazi Germany and set up his practice in New York in the mid-1930s. Like Jacobson, he had some celebrity patients, who included Jackie Kennedy toward the latter part of her life, jazz great Charlie Parker, and the Beatles. Like Jacobson, both Bishop and Freymann lost their licenses in 1975 after they were exposed by the *New York Times*. This was one of the great medical scandals of the 1970s and became one of the causa belli for Richard Nixon's War on Drugs, which continues unabated today

One of the stories circulating about Max Jacobson's second wife, Nina Hagen, was that the doctor murdered her because of an alleged affair she had with JFK's college roommate, Chuck Spalding. According to the story, Nina began having an affair with Spalding, which resulted in the breakup of Mr. Spalding's marriage. Many blame the affair on the fact that both were addicted to Max's injections of amphetamine.

Was it jealousy that led Max to eliminate Nina gradually, but intentionally, or was Max just carelessly dispensing his drugs to her? Alan Jay Lerner's assistant and Jacobson patient Doris Shapiro remembered the death of Nina in her book *We Danced All Night*: "One night Max and his wife, Nina, came to the Waldorf offices [of Alan Jay Lerner]. We were sitting around the large upholstered room while Max fussed with his bag, when suddenly Nina said softly, 'I don't feel well.' Max heard her and began to prepare a syringe. 'No, Max,' she said. 'No more.'

"'Come,' he said coddlingly. 'I'll make you feel better.' He took her into another room, holding the syringe. After they came out, she sat quietly, saying, 'Yes, thank you.' She felt better."[84]

Shapiro wrote that she learned a week later that Nina was dead. Shapiro noted that once Nina entered the hospital, she was beyond Max's ability to treat her, because he had no hospital affiliations. Shapiro later recalled meeting one of Max's "nurses" named

Beatrice. Shapiro asked her what had happened to Nina. Beatrice looked very sad, "crestfallen," Shapiro remembered, and revealed, "I'm afraid Max did it." She asked Beatrice how the hospital listed Nina's cause of death. "Oh, they said some virus or something, I don't know,"[85] Doris said Beatrice told her. But when she asked whether the hospital had performed an autopsy, Beatrice answered that there was no request for one.

Alvin Aronson, who was an Alan Jay Lerner associate, had a clear recognition of the event Doris Shapiro described in her book. He said, "I was shocked that Nina had passed away. . . . When Max came into the offices the next day, I was flabbergasted. . . . He had a strange look upon his face . . . almost a look of contentment."[86]

Michael Samek disputed Shapiro's and Aronson's accounts, recalling that Max "couldn't stand funerals. Nina's death was traumatic for him. She died in the early 1960s. The night when his wife was dying, I stayed up with him half the night composing a letter to JFK, which he never sent. It was all happening at once."[87] But, ultimately, it was all about the drugs, which he continued to dispense after Nina's death.

Jacobson's unregulated distribution and manufacture of amphetamines slowed after his lab was raided by the Federal Bureau of Narcotics in 1965 and his material was removed. However, as there was no federal law under which to prosecute Jacobson, the Bureau's action was essentially toothless. Max sued the Narcotic Bureau, and no records exist to indicate whether Max's suit was settled.

Prior to 1970, there were many ambiguous laws and attempts at self-policing by each state's medical boards. President Richard Nixon sought to remedy this situation, which ended when the Controlled Substances Act (CSA) was enacted into law as Title II of the Comprehensive Drug Abuse Prevention and Control Act of 1970.

The CSA became the federal US drug policy under which the manufacture, importation, possession, use, and distribution of certain substances is regulated. The Act also served as the national implementing legislation for the Single Convention on Narcotic Drugs. Amphetamines were originally placed under Controlled Substances-Schedule III, but moved to Schedule II in 1971 because of their addictive nature; however, injectable methamphetamine had always been on the Controlled Substances-Schedule II. Schedule II substances were not banned or made illegal, such as those on Schedule I, which includes marijuana; however, Schedule II substances have the following attributes:

1. The drug or other substances have a high potential for abuse.

2. The drug or other substances have currently accepted medical use in treatment in the United States, or currently accepted medical use with severe restrictions.

3. Abuse of the drug or other substances may lead to severe psychological or physical dependence.

Whatever the final verdict on Jacobson—whether he was a misunderstood healer who made his patients feel good or a meth addict who himself suffered from the psychotic effects of the drug—we do know that a number of his patients suffered under his treatment. How he kept both Marilyn Monroe and John F. Kennedy addicted, and destroyed the highest point of Mickey Mantle's career, attests to Max's near-psychotic desperation to control others. He was responsible—either directly or indirectly—for the death of his own wife, Mark Shaw, and Bob Richardson. And while he claimed altruism, he was manufacturing drugs without FDA approval in a lab that never passed any inspections while it shipped methamphetamine compounds all over the world.

All of this would eventually catch up with Max Jacobson when he became the subject of a *New York Times* exposé. Ultimately, Max would face his own "final days."

Max Jacobson Patient List

(from office records supplied by Ruth Jacobson, courtesy of the
C. David Heymann Archive)

Alan Jay Lerner

Alice Ghostley*

Anais Nin

Andy Warhol

Andy Williams*

Anthony Quinn

Arlene Francis

Arnold Saint-Subber

Billy Wilder*

Bob Cummings*

Bob Fosse

Bob Richardson

Burgess Meredith

Burton Lane

Cary Grant

Cecil B. DeMille

Chuck Spalding

Cicely Tyson

Claude Pepper

Doris Shapiro

Dorothy McGuire

Eddie Albert

Eddie Fisher*

Edie Sedgewick

Edward G. Robinson

Elizabeth Taylor*

Ellen Hanley

Elvis Presley

Emilio Pucci

Eusebio Morales

Everly Bros.

Felice Orlandi

Franchot Tone

Franco Zefferelli

Frank Sinatra

George Kaufman

Gore Vidal

Greta Stuckles

Gypsy Rose Lee (Rose Havoc)

Harry S. Truman

Hedy Lamarr

Henry and June Miller

Henry Morgan

Hermione Gingold

Howard Cosell

Hugh Martin

Igor Goran

Igor Stravinsky

Ingrid Bergman	Mickey Mantle
Jacqueline Kennedy	Mickey Mantle
Jerry Lewis*	Mike Todd
John F. Kennedy	Milton Blackstone
John Hancock (director)	Nancy Olson
John Murray Anderson	Nelson Rockefeller
Johnny Mathis	Niels Bohr
Jose Ferrer	Otto Preminger
Josh Logan	Pat Suzuki*
Judith Exner Campbell	Patrick O'Neil
Judy Garland	Paul Lynde
Katherine Dunham	Paul Robeson
Kay Thompson	Peter Lawford
Kurt Braun	Peter Lorre
Lee Bouvier Radziwill*	Phyllis McGuire*
Leonard Bernstein	Rebekah Harkness
Leonard Silman	Rex Harrison
Leontyne Price	Richard Burton
Louis Nizer	Richard M. Nixon
Mabel Mercer	Rita Moreno
Margaret Leighton	Robert Goulet
Marianne Anderson	Rod Serling
Marilyn Monroe	Roddy McDowell*
Marion Marlowe	Ronny Graham
Mark Shaw	Rosalind Russell
Marlene Dietrich	Roscoe Lee Browne*
Martin Gabel	Rosemary Clooney
Maya Deren	Roy Cohn
Maynard Ferguson	Sam "MoMo" Giancanna
Mel Allen	Sharon Tate

Shelley Winters
Spiro Agnew
Stash Radziwill
Stavros Niachros
Tennessee Williams
Tom Parker
Tony Curtis*
Tony Franciosa
Truman Capote

Van Cliburn
Vic Damone
Vincent Alo ("Jimmy Blue
    Eyes")
Winston Churchill
Yul Brynner
Zero Mostel

*Interviewed

Endnotes

1 RAL Mike Samek interview, 1/07
2 Copy of Letitia Baldrige
3 Samek Interview, RAL
4 IRAL interview with Alice Ghostley, 2007
5 RAL Samek interview
6 *Been There, Done That*, by Eddie Fisher and David Fisher, pp. 55-57
7 Jackie Barbara Leaming, 155
8 Leaming, Jackie, pp. 478
9 Eddie Fisher interview, 2007 RAL
10 Capote, http://gorightly.wordpress.com/2007/11/25/when-camelot-grooved/
11 Doris Shapiro, pp. 166-167
12 Shapiro, pp. 235-238
13 Max Jacobson's diaries
14 ibid
15 ibid
16 ibid
17 ibid
18 ibid
19 Patience Abbe, *Around the World in Eleven Years*, 1936, pp. 175-176
20 Mike Samek interview, RAL 1/07
21 http://amphetamines.com/nazi.html, "Hitler's Drugged Soldiers," Andreas Ulrich
22 "Hitler's Drugged Soldiers," Ulrich
23 "Hitler's Drugged Soldiers," Ulrich
24 Max Jacobson's diaries

25 Max Jacobson's diaries
1 *The Selfish Gene*, Oxford University Press, 1976
2 Michael Samek, private interview, 1/12/2007
3 Private Interview, 4/30/2007
4 Cambridge, Oxford University Press, 2008
5 Lexing, University of Kentucky Press, 1993
6 New York: the Swallow Press, Harcourt, 1967
7 Interview with Mike Samek, 2007
8 New York: Simon & Schuster, 2010
9 Interview with Billy Wilder, July, 1995
10 *Tennessee Williams: A Memoir,* New York: Bantam, 1976, p 225
11 Scott Eyman, *Empire of Dreams: The Life of Cecil B. DeMille, New York:* Simon & Schuster, 2010
12 ibid
13 Private interview with Valentina Quinn, July 2007
14 Max Jacobson's diaries
15 Private Interview, October, 2012
16 Private Interview, March, 2006
17 Private Interview, June, 2011
18 Private Interview, March, 2006
19 Private Interview with George Clooney July, 2007
20 Prentice-Hall, 1960
21 Private Interview with Dwayne

179

Hickman, February, 2007
22 Private Interview with Art Linkletter, April, 2007
23 Interview with Bob Finkel, June, 2005
24 Private Interview, 2008
25 Private Interview, March, 2007
26 Private Interview, November 1996
27 Private Interview, March 1996
28 Private Interview, March, 2007
29 Private Interview, March, 2006
30 *Mickey Mantle: The Last Boy and the End of America's Childhood,* New York: HarperCollins, 2010
31 ibid
32 Curt Smith, The Voice: *Mel Allen's Untold Story,* New York: Lyons Press, 2007
33 New York: The World Publishing Company, 1970
34 *Sixty-One: The Team, the Record, the Men* by Terry Pluto and Tony Kubek, (New York: Fireside, 1989)
35 Private Letter, 11/15/2012
36 November, 2010
37 Private Interview, August, 2006
38 New York: Three Rivers Press, 2000
39 Private Interview, August 2006
40 New York: Random House, 2004
41 *Time* magazine, May 24, 1962
42 Dorithy Kilgallen, "Maybe You Didn't Know," *The New American,* October 2, 1964
43 Private Interview, August, 2006
44 Private Interview, August, 2006
45 Private Interview, November, 2012
46 Skyhorse, 2012
47 Private Interview with David Heymann, November, 2009
48 Private Interview, December, 2012
49 *Choice People: The Greats, Near-Greats, and Ingrates I Have Known,* New York: Morrow, 1984
50 ibid
51 ibid
52 Private Interview with A.E. Hotchner, Movember, 2012
53 ibid
54 ibid
55 ibid
56 ibid
57 ibid
58 ibid
59 ibid
60 ibid
61 ibid
62 ibid
63 ibid
64 ibid
65 ibid
66 *Choice People: The Greats, Near-Greats, and Ingrates I Have Known* (New York: Morrow, 1984)
67 New York State Archives, Cultural Education Center, Board of Regents, 4/25/1975
68 ibid
69 Private Interview, 7/15/07
70 ibid
71 Private Interview, 7/15/07

[72] *NYT*, December 4, 1972, by Boyce Rensenberger with contribution by Jane Brody and Lawrence Altman

[73] December, 1973

[74] New York State Archives, Cultural Education Center, Board of Medical Education, 4/25/1975

[75] *NYT*, 4/26/1975

[76] Private Interview, August, 2006

[77] Private Interview, March 2006

[78] Private Interview, November 2010

[79] Private Interview March, 2007

[80] Alvin Aronson Private Interview, November, 2012

[81] New York State Archives, Cultural Education Center, Board of Medicine 4/25/1975

[82] ibid

[83] *NYT* 12/4/1972 by Boyce Rensenberger

[84] *We Danced All Night*, New York: Random House, 1995

[85] ibid

[86] Private Interview with Alvin Aronson, November, 2012

[87] Private Interview, August, 2006

Interviews

The Authors wish to thank those listed below in helping this book become a reality and sharing their wisdom and thoughts.

The following interviews were held in person, on the telephone or through e—mail between January 2005 and December 2012.

Alan Young—actor
Alice Ghostley—actress
Alvin Aronson—Playwright, patient/friend of Dr. Jacobson
Andy Williams—singer, tv host
Ann B. Davis—actress
Annika Bjork, film historian—Sweden
Art Linkletter—television host, author
Austin "Rocky" Kalish—television writer
Barbara Hall—research archivist at Motion Picture Academy/Margaret Herrick Library
Barry Grauman—television historian
Bea Schwartz Heymann—writer
Bernard Slade—playwright, television writer
Bill Berle—son of Milton Berle
Bill Cunningham—radio and television talk show host
Billy Wilder—film director, screenwriter
Bob Newhart—television comedian
Boyce Rensberger—journalist
Brooke Garson—Producer
C. David Heymann— author
Carol Summers—film executive
Charles Nadler—executive
Chris Costello—daughter of Lou Costello

Curt Smith—author and speechwriter
David Shaw—archivist, author
Del Reisman—writer, producer
Diana McGarvey—researcher
Dorothy Johnson—actress
Dr. Bradford A. Pressman
Dr. David Simons—astronaut, physician
Dr. Jeffrey Kelman—physician, author
Dr. Kim Cameron—Dean of Business, University of Michigan
Dr. Lawrence Altman—physician, journalist
Dr. Lawrence Hatterer—psychiatrist, treated JFK
Dr. Leslie K. Iverson—author, Professor of Pharmacology at Oxford University, UK
Dr. Myra Hatterer—psychiatrist
Dr. Robert Dallek—historian, author
Dr. Thomas Jacobson—cardiologist, son of Max Jacobson
Dwayne Hickman—actor
Ed Asner—actor
Eddie Carroll—actor
Eddie Fisher—singer
Eddie Kritzer—television producer
Eileen Wesson—actress
Frank Bank—actor

Frank Cullen—film historian
Fred Westbock—agent
Frederick Kempe—author, journalist and President of Atlantic Council
Gary Owens—television and radio performer
George Cukor—film director
George Greely—composer
Gerald Clarke—author
Gore Vidal—author
Gregory Jackson—archivist
Hal Kanter—film director, writer, producer
Hank Messick—author ("Silent Syndicate")
Herbie Pilato—author
Irma Kalish—television writer
Irving Brecher—writer
Jake Schultz—author
Jamie Farr—actor
Jane Brody—journalist, author
Jane Leavy—journalist, author
Jason Wingreen—actor
Jay Kanter—agent
Jeanette Seaver—publisher
Jeff Jonas—television historian
Jenni Matz—Archive of American Television
Jerry Lewis—film comedian
Jill Jacobson—daughter of Max Jacobson
Joan Howard Maurer—daughter of Moe Howard
Joan Roberts Hickman—actress
Joey Bishop—actor, comic
Judy Jashinsky—artist
Julie Eichhorst—FBI
Julie Newmar—actress, author

Juliet Cumings Shaw—archivist, artist, author
Ken McKnight—official at Dept. of Commerce
Larry Flynt—Publisher
Larry Gelbart—writer
Larry King—TV talk show host
Laura Leff—curator of Jack Benny estate
Laurel Cummings Jones—daughter of Bob Cummings
Leonard Maltin
Leonard Stern—producer, writer, publisher
Lincoln Ware—Talk Show Host
Linda Henning—actress
Linda Jay Geldens—author
Lois Linkletter—writer
Lon Davis—film historian
Lori Saunders—actress
Mark Evanier—television writer, historian
Matthew Jacobson—grandson of Max Jacobson
Max Baer, Jr.—actor
Max Diamond—convicted 'bootlegger"
Melinda Cummings Cameron—daughter of Bob Cummings
Michael Samek—decorated War hero, executive, friend of Max Jacobson
Michelle Cummings— daughter of Bob Cummings
Milton Berle—TV host, comedian (interview was in 1995)
Monte Aidem—comedy writer (*Tonight Show*)
Nancy Reagan—First Lady

Ned Comstock—USC Film and Television Archives
Nigel Hamilton—historian, author
Nina Burleigh—journalist and author
Norman Brokaw—agent, former Chairman of William Morris Agency
Pamela Shoop—actress
Pat Suzuki—actress/singer
Patricia Cummings—daughter of Bob Cummings
Patty Andrews—singer (Andrew Sisters)
Paul Landis—Eisenhower and Kennedy Secret Service Agent
Paul Sheffrin—publicist
Phyllis McGuire—singer
Rachel Lansing (Joi)—actress
Reinhart Peschke—Cinematographer
Richard Reeves—historian, journalist, author
Richard Seaver—publisher
Robert "Bob" Easton—actor, director
Robert "Bob" Finkel—television producer
Robert Child, film director
Robert Cummings, Jr.— son of Bob Cummings
Robert Osborne—television host, journalist, actor
Robin Klein—actress
Roddy McDowell—actor
Roger Rapoport—author, journalist
Ron Palumbo—film historian

Roscoe Lee Browne—actor
Rose Marie—actress
Ruth Jacobson—wife of Max Jacobson
Sam Denoff
Sam Irvin—film director, author
Seymour Hersh—journalist, author
Shawn Levy—author, film critic
Sheila James Kuehl—actress and State Senator
Sheldon Keller—TV Writer
Sid Caesar—TV Host, actor
Sidney Omar—astrologer
Stanley Frazen—film editor
Stone "Bud" Widney—Broadway Producer (with Alan Jay Lerner)
Stuart Shostak—television historian
Tania Grossinger—author
Ted Wionicek—writer
Terry Pluto—sports columnist, author
Thomas Putnam—Director of the Kennedy Museum
Tom Claire—television historian
Toni Bradlee—socialite
Tony Curtis—actor, author
Tracy Hotchner—animal activist, radio host
Valentina Quinn—actress, author
Van Cliburn
Vicki Bronstein—publicist
Vicki Lawrence—actress
Wallace Seawell—photographer
William Asher—film and television director
William Schallert—actor

Bibliography

Altman M.D., Lawrence. "The Doctor's World: Very Real Questions for Fictional President." *New York Times*, October 9, 2001.

Belafonte, Harry, and Schnaverson, Michael. *My Song: a Memoir.* New York: Knopf, 2011.

Brody, Jane. "Patient and His Doctor: Quandary for Medicine." *New York Times*, January 16, 1973.

Bureau of Narcotic and Dangerous Drugs. "Report :Dr. Max Jacobson." 1959-1979. Acquired as part of findings resulting from authors request for information using the "Freedom of Information Act" (FOIA).

Burroughs-Hannsberry. *Karen. Bad Boys: The Actors of the Film Noir.* New York: McFarland, 2008.

Carlson, Peter. "Jack Kennedy and Dr. Feelgood." *American History* 46, no. 2 (2011): 30.

Clarke, Gerald. *Capote: A Biography.* New York: Simon and Schuster, 2010.

Clifford, Laura, and Robin. Review of *In The Mirror of Maya Deren.* ReelingReviews.com, 2010.

Curtis, Tony, and Vieira, Mark. *The Making of Some Like it Hot.* Wiley Books, 2009.

Curtis, Tony, and Golenbock, Peter. *An American Prince: A Memoir.* New York: Crown Archetype, 2008.

Dallek, Robert. *An Unfinished Life: John F. Kennedy 1917-1963.* Back Bay Books, 2004.

Eyman, Scott. *The Empire of Dreams. The Epic Life of Cecil B. DeMille.* New York: Simon & Shuster, 2010.

Fisher, David, and Fisher, Eddie. *Been There Done That.* New York: Hutchinson Press, 1999.

Fisher, Eddie. *My Life, My Loves.* New York: Harper Collins, 1984.

Gentry, Curt. *J. Edgar Hoover: The Man and his Secrets.* New York: W. W. Norton & Co., 2001.

Grossinger, Tania. *Growing Up At Grossingers.* New York: Skyhorse Publishing, 2008.

Hamilton, George. *George Hamilton: Don't Mind If I Do: My Adventures In Hollywood.* JR Books Ltd., 2009.

Hersh, Seymour M. *The Dark Side of Camelot.* Back Bay Books, 1998.

Heymann, C. David. *A Woman Called Jackie.* New York: Lyle Stuart, 1989.

Heymann, C. David. *Bobby and Jackie: A Love Story.* New York: Atria Books, 2009.

Hill, Clint, and McCubbin, Lisa. *Mrs. Kennedy and Me.* New York: Gallery Books, 2012.

Hotchner, A.E. *Choice People: The Greats, Near Greats and Ingrates I have Known.* New York: William Morrow and Co., 1984.

Irvin, Sam. *Kay Thompson: From Funny Face to Eloise.* New York: Simon & Schuster, 2011.

Iverson, Dr. Leslie K. *Speed, Ecstasy, Ritalin: The Science of Amphetamines.* New York: Oxford University Press, 2008.

Jacobson M.D., Max. "A Doctor's Advice to the Bewildered." *Cromwell Magazine,* 1968.

Kauppila, Jean L., and Paietta, Ann Catherine. *Health Professionals on Screen.* Scarecrow Press, 1999.

Kempe, Frederick. *Berlin 1961: Kennedy, Khrushchev and the Most Dangerous Place on Earth.* Berkeley Trade, 2012.

Leamer, Larry. *The Kennedy Men 1901-1963.* New York: William Morrow, 2002.

Leaming, Barbara. *Mrs. Kennedy: The Missing History of the Kennedy Years.* New York: Free Press, 2002.

Leaming, Barbara. *Marilyn Monroe.* Three Rivers Press, 2000.

Leary, Timothy. *Leary on Drugs: New Material from the Archives! Advice, Humor and Wisdom from the Godfather of Psychedelia.* Re/Search Publications, 2009.

Lerman, Leo, and Pascall, Stephen. *The Grand Surprise: The Journals of Leo Lerman.* New York: Knopf, 2007.

Leavy, Jane. *The Last Boy: Mickey Mantle and the End of America's Childhood.* New York: Harper Perennial, 2011.

Loog-Oldham, Andrew. *Stoned: A Memoir of London in the 1960s.* New York: St. Martin's Press, 2001.

Mandell, Arnold. *The Nightmare Season.* New York: Random House, 1976.

Mann, Theodore. *Journeys in the Night: Creating a New America.* Applause, 2009.

Marshall, David. *The DD Group: An Online Investigation Into the Death of Marilyn Monroe.* iUniverse, Inc., 2005.

"Medicine: Bogomolets & the Longer Life," June 17, 1946, www.time.com/time/magazine/article/0,9171,793116,00.html.

Neumeyer, Kathleen. "Tragedy of Elizabeth Taylor." *Correspondence Magazine.* January 1960.

New York State Archives. Series 17267 and Series 17265-Board of Regents, 124 pp.

Nin, Anais. *The Diary of Anaïs Nin 1934-1939.* Mariner Books, 1969.

Park, Bert E. *Ailing, Aging, Addicted: Studies of Compromised Leadership.* University of Kentucky Press, 1993.

Plimpton, George, and Stein, Jean. *Edie: American Girl.* Grove Press, 1994.

Plummer, Christopher. *In Spite of Myself.* Vintage Books, 2012.

Rapoport, Roger. *The Super Doctors.* New York: Playboy Press, 1977.

Reeves, Richard. "Kennedy's Private Ills." *New York Times,* November 21, 2002.

Reeves, Richard. *President Kennedy: Profile of Power.* New York: Simon & Schuster, 1994.

Rensberger, Boyce et al. "Amphetamines Used By New York Physician..." *New York Times,* December 4, 1972.

Safire, William. "Kennedy Agonistes." *New York Times,* November 18, 2002.

Schwartz, Susan. *Into the Unknown: The Remarkable Life of Dr. Hans Kraus.* iUniverse, Inc., 2005.

Shapiro, Doris. *We Danced All Night: My Life Behind the Scenes With Alan Jay Lerner.* New York: Barricade Books, 1993.

Smith, Sally Bedell. *Grace and Power: The Private World of the Kennedy White House.* New York: Random House, Inc., 2004.

Spoto, Donald. *Jacqueline Bouvier Kennedy Onassis: A Life.* New York: St. Martins, 2000.

Travell, Janet. *Office Hours Day and Night.* New York: World Publishing Company, 1968.

Vidal, Gore. *Point to Navigation: A Memoir.* Vintage Press, 2007.

Waters, John, and Williams, Tennessee. *Memoirs.* New Directions, 2006.

Williams. Tennessee. "Letter to the Editor." *New York Times,* December 12, 1972.

Index

Hotchner, A. E., 141–146

I
Infectious austeomyelitis, 33
Isophan, 51
Iversen, Leslie, 64, 65

J
Jacobson, Louis, 26, 27
Jacobson, Max
    addiction to methamphetamines,
        45, 65, 145, 166
    BNDD raid of office, 147
    celebrity patients of, 66
    in Czechoslovakia, 55–57
    as diagnostician, 41
    family of, 25–27
    FBI surveillance of office, 8, 9
    impact of life and practices of, 3–4
    influence in entertainment industry,
        75–89
    influence on DeMille, 66–74
    interest in biochemistry, 41, 47
    KGB raid of office, 92, 99
    as medical assistant, 32, 33
    medical internship with Bier,
        41–43, 47
    medical license revocation, 66, 146,
        159–162, 166
    medical studies, 38–43
    in Paris, 58–60
    practice in Berlin, 45–54
    practice in Manhattan, 61
    relationship with Kennedy, 91–103
    research on methamphetamine, 49
    study of multiple sclerosis, 63
Jacobson, Thomas, 83, 115
Johnson, Lyndon B., 16, 126, 128, 132,
    133, 135, 138
Jung, Carl, 45–47

K
Kalish, Austin "Rocky," 76, 77
Kennedy, Bobby, 115, 118, 119, 121–
    123, 130, 132
Kennedy, Jackie, 101, 116, 157, 158,
    166, 170
Kennedy, Jacqueline, 97
Kennedy, John Fitzgerald
    assassination of, 134–136, 139
    code name of, 7
    debate with Nixon, 21
    illnesses, 12, 13, 16, 17
    inauguration, 21–22
    injections of methamphetamine, 8,
        10, 18–20, 95, 97, 98, 101, 102,
        124–125
    manic condition of, 125–128
    meeting with Khrushchev, 25, 91,
        97–100
    meeting with McMillan, 100, 101
    Vienna Summit, 91–103
Kennedy, Robert, 9, 111, 127, 166, 167
Khrushchev, Nikita, 91, 92, 97–99, 128
Khrushchev, Nina, 97

L
Landis, Paul, 134, 137
Lavan, Harvey, 143
Lawford, Peter, 121
Leavy, Jane, 107, 108
Lowner, Alice, 44, 45, 56
LSD, 132, 140

M
Mann, Harvey, 141, 142–146, 159
Mantle, Mickey Charle, 105–110
McKnight, Ken, 9
Methamphetamines, 4, 5, 8, 10, 18–20,
    62, 95, 101, 102, 112
    effects of, 10, 18, 19, 49, 50
    as mood enhancer, 46, 63
    side effects of, 64, 79, 121, 124
    use in German military, 51–52